Guiding Advanced Readers in Middle School

By Teresa Smith Masiello

Great Potential Press®
www.giftedbooks.com

Guiding Advanced Readers in Middle School

Edited by: Jennifer Ault
Interior design: The Printed Page
Cover design: Hutchison-Frey

Published by Great Potential Press, Inc.
7025 1st Avenue, Suite 5
Scottsdale, AZ 85251

Printed and bound in the United States of America using partially recycled paper.

Great Potential Press and associated logos are trademarks and/or registered trademarks of Great Potential Press, Inc.

14 13 12 11 10   5 4 3 2 1

At the time of this book's publication, all facts and figures cited are the most current available. All telephone numbers, addresses, and website URLs are accurate and active; all publications, organizations, websites, and other resources exist as described in this book; and all have been verified as of the time this book went to press. The author(s) and Great Potential Press make no warranty or guarantee concerning the information and materials given out by organizations or content found at websites, and we are not responsible for any changes that occur after this book's publication. If you find an error or believe that a resource listed here is not as described, please contact Great Potential Press.

Library of Congress Cataloging-in-Publication Data

Masiello, Teresa Smith, 1962-
   Guiding advanced readers in middle school / by Teresa Smith Masiello.
      p. cm.
   ISBN-13: 978-1-935067-01-6
   ISBN-10: 1-935067-01-X
   1. Reading (Middle school) 2. Language arts (Middle school) 3. English language—Composition and exercises—Study and teaching. 4. Effective teaching. I. Title.
   LB1632.M295 2010
   371.95'34—dc22
                              2010033431

Dedication

This book is dedicated to my parents, Marshall and Cecilia Smith.
Their continued support taught me to always "climb that mountain"
and never give up, because when you give up, you create your own roadblock.
This book gives proof that the climb might not always be an easy one,
but the lessons along the way certainly make reaching the top fulfilling.

Contents

List of Reproducible Forms

List of Charts

Please note that the activities in Chapters 4 and 5 can be copied and used.

Acknowledgments

This book would not be possible if not for the continued support of my family and friends. Sitting at my computer as days turned into nights was not only difficult for me, but for my family as well. Thank you to my husband, Paul; he cooked many dinners so I could make final edits. A big thank-you to Anthony, Jacob, and Nicole; their support and patience allowed me to conduct research while spending time at the local library. I am sure they will be happy when their mom can attend football and softball games without bringing along a large tote bag filled with articles and scrap paper.

A heartfelt thank-you must go to Janet Gore and Jim Webb. Their belief in this book has opened many doors in my life. Even when my computer and our home were attacked by strange viruses, Jan remained calm and sent her support for everyone to get better. Jan and Jen Ault's edits have made this book much more readable and usable, and Jen's attention to detail was phenomenal. Great Potential Press truly believes in doing what is best for gifted students and strives to publish quality resource materials that help parents and teachers best meet the academic, social, and emotional needs of gifted individuals.

Finally, I would like to thank my friends and teachers who allowed me to field test the many activities and strategies found in this book. I am sure it was not easy having to change lesson plans so that I could take over their classrooms.

I refer to "opening the door" in this book. I am blessed to have so many people who stand by me, waiting to turn the knob so that I can "walk through the door."

Preface

From your parents you learn love and laughter and how to put one foot before the other. But when books are opened you discover you have wings.

~Helen Hayes

As the mother of a gifted teenage son and a teacher of gifted and talented students, I know that the pre-teen and teen years can be difficult and confusing—both for young teens and for the adults who live and work with them. I have watched my son carry himself one day with dignity and self-confidence, only to wake up the next day to find him tearing his bedroom apart as he searches for a backpack that was apparently abducted by aliens. I have participated in adult-like conversations with him about his school day on Monday, and then on Tuesday notice that he can no longer speak in complete sentences when I ask, "How was school today?"

The need to search for his belongings, along with a periodic lapse in verbal communication skills, has led me to believe that my son is actually searching for something else, something more significant than his backpack and more productive than our conversations together. Why does he want to be alone one day and with friends the next? Why is he not reading books for pleasure anymore? Why is he not achieving in his classes? How can I better understand what he is searching for or what he is going through during this time of adolescent growth?

Teaching and raising gifted children both require a variety of resources. It is important to understand that gifted students in middle school have certain characteristics that make life more difficult for them as they experience changes in social, emotional, and intellectual development. Not only are they dealing with the typical hormonal changes of puberty and the social issues that come with this stage of adolescence, but they are often facing academic concerns as well. They may excel in school, or they may not. They may fit in well with classmates, or they may not. But one thing is typically true for all of them: unless the standard middle school curriculum is altered for them in some way, they will not find it challenging or engaging, and they will suffer from boredom, frustration, and perhaps a host of other problems, including underachievement.

One way in which to help these adolescents is by providing plenty of well-chosen books that feature complex characters who experience many of the same struggles that our gifted teens face on a daily basis. Gifted adolescents can identify with these characters and learn that others have faced similar challenges and have been able to surmount them. Reading programs that contain intellectually challenging books, combined with appropriately planned discussions, enable gifted teens to identify and apply important coping strategies to their own lives. As teachers introduce students to quality literature, they will see immediate changes in the students' attitudes toward learning and achievement in reading. These books will not only help meet students' intellectual needs, but also help to enhance their social and emotional growth.

In her book *Some of My Best Friends Are Books* (3rd Edition, 2009), Judith Halsted says:

> *Stories help us guide the emotional development of our gifted children*
> *when they touch the emotions. A skillful author can make us care*
> *about characters who have the same problems…. If a book can "hook"*
> *a child emotionally, she may be far more receptive to ideas than if they*
> *are presented in a lecture by a concerned adult.* (pp. 44-45)

Years of watching teenagers and talking with teachers of gifted adolescents have changed my views about middle school students forever; I now look at this age group through a completely different lens. When I first taught gifted students in grades 6-8, I didn't understand the needs of gifted adolescents. I didn't understand the importance of using great books and great literature with these students. Though I don't claim to have all the answers (Who does for teenagers?!), I have learned some things that I think may help others.

Guiding Advanced Readers in Middle School is for teachers, parents, administrators, and counselors of adolescent gifted students. My earlier book, *Literature Links: Activities for Gifted Readers*, focused on students in grades K-5. This book focuses on gifted students in grades 6-8. When curriculum does not match their needs and abilities, middle school students become frustrated. We can help by choosing literature based on specific criteria relating to giftedness.

Dedicated teachers want to challenge their gifted students, even when resources are minimal. Attentive parents search for ways to help monitor their child's academic, social, and emotional progress in school. Most administrators agree that meeting the needs of gifted students is sometimes difficult, because when state and local funds are cut, gifted education typically takes a large portion of the cut. Yet gifted readers continue to show up at school, ready to learn, ready to read, and ready to be challenged. They deserve to have interesting books to read—books that match their reading ability, and books that they will learn from.

As I reflect on those involved in the education of gifted students, many questions come to mind. How much longer can teachers be expected to meet the needs of all ability levels with limited materials? How much longer will parents have to search for ways to help their gifted adolescents? When will administrators have the freedom to make choices that will serve to protect and enhance the education of gifted students? When will the doors promising new and challenging learning be open to them?

Reflecting on my own gifted teen and my 21 years of teaching experience, I am thankful to all who helped me see the importance of using quality literature with gifted teens. Let's give these students wings; let's give them well-chosen books that help them spread those wings and fly! I hope this book will help. Happy reading!

About This Book

Students, teachers, parents, and school administrators can all benefit from reading this book. It provides a framework to meet the needs of gifted readers in heterogeneous classrooms in middle school, and it includes information on differentiating instruction, as well as an extensive list of activities and strategies that can be integrated into regular classrooms that contain gifted readers.

Student Objectives

As gifted students gain exposure to good books, they will begin to realize how appropriately selected literature can help them with the personal struggles they face because of their age and abilities. Students will:

➤ Learn to identify and deal with personal issues
➤ Learn how to select literature that is appropriate for their age group
➤ Be able to empathize with students in their peer group
➤ Learn to recognize and appreciate other cultures and societies
➤ Be able to share in the responsibility of their education

Teacher Objectives

When teachers use the strategies and activities suggested in this book, they will begin to better meet the needs of their gifted readers. Teachers will:

➤ Learn to identify characteristics and needs of gifted readers in middle school

➤ Learn to appreciate and value gifted adolescents and what they bring to classrooms

➤ Understand that gifted adolescents need guidance when selecting appropriate reading material in order to fulfill their educational, social, and emotional needs

➤ Understand that gifted readers need opportunities to go beyond the regular curriculum because they possess large vocabularies, along with excellent processing and problem-solving skills

➤ Be able to enhance motivation for gifted adolescents who are underachieving in their classrooms

➤ Learn ways to effectively communicate with students and their parents

➤ Become knowledgeable about the many different ways in which to assess students

Parent Objectives

As parents of gifted adolescents learn more about their children, they can help them engage in more effective learning and social situations. Parents will:

➤ Be able to apply research to issues that their child might be dealing with on a daily basis

➤ Understand the importance of using books to help gifted students adjust to specific situations

> ➤ Be able to evaluate trade books so that content is relevant and appropriate for their child

> ➤ Learn how to effectively get information from teachers when they have questions about their child's learning

> ➤ Understand ways in which teachers assess gifted readers in their classrooms

Administrator Objectives

Administrators who implement the strategies and ideas in this book will help make curriculum in their buildings more suitable for gifted adolescents. Administrators will:

> ➤ Appreciate why it is important to remain involved in the education of gifted middle school students

> ➤ Learn how books can help gifted adolescents as they struggle to find ways to fit in with their peers

> ➤ Recognize that there are many resources available to help gifted adolescents

> ➤ Understand the need for more differentiated lessons in classrooms containing gifted readers

> ➤ Be able to evaluate the performance of classroom teachers as they provide instruction for gifted readers

> ➤ Be able to share in the positive outcomes when teachers and gifted readers integrate appropriate trade books in their classrooms

Overview of Chapters

While all of the chapters in this book build upon one another to show a progression in meeting the needs of gifted readers in middle school, some chapters contain specific information that is directed to certain populations. Here is a preview of the chapters.

Chapter 1 looks at the world of gifted adolescents and the problems they face because of their distinct characteristics, exploring some of these characteristics in both their positive and negative aspects. It also identifies concerns that are often evident among adolescent gifted readers, such as feeling different from their peers, trying to hide their giftedness, attempting to be perfect in all things, underachieving, and exhibiting social and emotional worries. This chapter describes these issues, as well as some ways in which to handle them.

Chapter 2 summarizes the importance of using quality literature with gifted adolescents and provides ways for adults to select books to help meet the needs of these students. This chapter is a great resource for parents and teachers who are looking for books that will challenge their gifted readers.

Chapter 3 contains a comprehensive list of instructional strategies that can be used with gifted readers in middle school, including such methods of differentiation as curriculum compacting, learning contracts, activity menus, and literature discussion groups. This chapter can actually be copied from this book and placed in teacher planning books.

It provides practical ways for teachers to challenge gifted students in the regular class-room, with detailed instructions for using each strategy.

Chapters 4 and 5 are all about the books! Four titles have been chosen, based on liter-ary elements appropriate for grades 6-8, to provide examples of how such books can be used. There are vocabulary words, reproducible activities, and higher-level questions for each title. These are the chapters that make the job of teaching middle school students easier. All middle school English teachers, even those who do not teach gifted students, will benefit from reading these chapters, as the content in them can be modified in order to meet the needs of all students—gifted students, high achievers, average students, and slower learners.

Chapter 6 includes ways to communicate with everyone involved in the process of educating middle school gifted readers. Communication is important at any level. How-ever, due to the lack of conversation and discussion that sometimes takes place with students during the adolescent years, it is important that teachers and parents communi-cate to help students achieve success.

Chapter 7 describes ways to assess gifted middle school students. Because differenti-ating instruction means tailoring lessons and activities to match the needs of students, it naturally follows that evaluations of these students should also be modified. This chapter will help classroom teachers properly assess their gifted students.

A Note about the Teachers: Throughout this book, the teachers are referred to in the feminine gender. This is for simplicity only, since we know that there are many good teachers who are men. Indeed, both male and female teachers who read this book will extract from it informa-tion and activities that will help them become more effective teachers of gifted readers.

Introduction

Teachers open the door, but you must enter by yourself.

~Chinese Proverb

Opening the Door

A group of gifted middle school students were asked to finish the phrase: "Opening the door means…." A sample of their written responses follows. Opening the door means:

➤ You must change your location.
➤ You have to close the door.
➤ You must first turn the knob.
➤ You know what is on the other side of the door.
➤ You have reached your destination.
➤ To leave your current location.
➤ You are home.
➤ You are ready to take the next step.
➤ Someone is getting a new opportunity in life.
➤ You have to start all over.
➤ To let someone in.
➤ To make a decision.

Many of the students in the group completed the phrase in quite literal ways. Not surprisingly, some of them connected their responses to events currently happening in their lives. However, gifted adolescents maintain viewpoints that are not always clear. What does a student mean when she says, "Opening the door means you have reached your destination"? Is she thinking about her future and where she is going in life? Or is she thinking about walking through the door to get to another location? What about the student who responded, "Opening the door means you have to start all over"? Is there something going on in this student's life that prompted this response? How about students who responded a certain way on Monday and then had a completely different response on Friday?

A brief discussion followed this assignment so that the students could consider and analyze their classmates' responses. As they talked, they found it interesting to note the differences and similarities in their responses, and to examine their own thinking styles. Many were surprised as they compared and contrasted responses that were literal with those that represented something more. This diverse group of students had created a list of statements that prompted them to think about ways in which we all think and respond differently to phrases and terms.

This activity was a wonderful tool for getting students to think and respond personally to an assignment while allowing them to be creative at the same time. Not only did it "open the door" to their minds, it also helped them uncover information about their own thinking. They could then examine different thinking styles, which prompted self-awareness. They began to make connections between thinking styles, learning, emotions, and behaviors. This led them to become excited about participating in their own learning. As a bonus, the students' discussion gave their teacher helpful information about individual students that she was able to apply as she created lessons for the future.

Integrating "Real" Instruction and Meaningful Curriculum

It was fascinating to watch the adolescents who participated in this activity analyze the responses of their fellow students. Although the activity did not take long, it provided "real" opportunities for the teacher and students. In other words, the students were able to connect the activity to real-life issues, and the lessons they learned from it were ones that they were then able to use in other applications of their learning. It is important at any grade level to provide gifted students with activities that are real and not so far "out of the box" that the students lose sight of the purpose of the assignment.

How many times do we, as educators, ask gifted students to complete banal activities, such as *Create a list of other uses for a pencil or a paperclip*, and consider them activities that require higher-level thinking? While this type of activity promotes flexibility, fluency, and open-ended, creative thinking, what use is it in the real world other than an enjoyable demonstration of brainstorming? Some students may perceive it as unworthy of their time. Gifted adolescents value their time; the last thing they want is to have their learning interrupted with meaningless activities.

Students are more willing to put forth effort when topics are interesting and assignments are meaningful. Assignments that encourage group discussion and promote open communication help students consider and appreciate different points of view. Gifted adolescents also need opportunities to expand their horizons while connecting to their own thoughts, feelings, and opinions. It is important that educators develop an understanding of gifted adolescent behaviors and needs so that they can enhance these students' educational experiences. To help meet the needs of all students in their classrooms, teachers also need access to a variety of resources and ideas as they develop curriculum.

Accommodating Gifted Readers in Middle School

The middle school environment does not always support gifted readers, even though it does routinely provide programs for students reading below grade level. Why is it not equally important to make accommodations for readers whose abilities are at the other end of the spectrum?

To find answers, we may need to ask some additional questions. Do educators embrace the belief that gifted readers need differentiated instruction? Do middle school teachers feel overwhelmed because of large populations of students with differing levels of ability? Is time an issue when differentiating instruction? Do teachers have the resources needed to provide appropriate instruction for gifted readers? Do teachers have access to quality literature that can be integrated into English programs?

Teachers who open the door to opportunities for their gifted students to read a variety of challenging, quality literature give those students a gift that they can use for the rest of their lives. But what happens if that door never opens? What if teachers choose *not* to provide quality literature and appropriate learning strategies for gifted readers? What happens if the door opens, but the student chooses not to walk through? What happens if the teacher provides differentiated strategies, but the gifted reader decides to become an underachiever? What happens if the gifted student walks through the open door and does not know what to do once he enters? And what happens if the gifted reader is ready and willing to put forth the additional effort but does not know how to begin the process? Gifted adolescents need guidance in their learning, and it is the responsibility of classroom teachers to provide that guidance and support.

Making Changes

Deciding to make changes to existing curriculum takes courage because it often means coming out of one's comfort zone. Such modifications also mean extra work and effort to successfully implement the changes.

Teachers can begin addressing issues often associated with adolescent gifted readers by examining their current curriculum and considering the following questions:

➤ What do I currently do with gifted readers that can be considered effective?

➤ What do I currently do with gifted readers that does not seem to be working?

➤ Have parents ever questioned the teaching methods I use with gifted readers? If so, were the questions related to management? Instruction?

➤ Does my administrator support the gifted program?

➤ Are there professional development opportunities where I can learn more?

➤ Do I truly know and understand the population of gifted adolescents?

3

Teaching Gifted Adolescents

Teaching at the middle school level can be rewarding and satisfying, as well as challenging and sometimes confusing. Our teachers are faced with the monumental task of providing instruction to students who often have widely varying degrees of ability. While school and governmental policies often serve the children in our classrooms who need extra assistance because of disabilities or impairments of one kind or another, they rarely reach out to the students who will most likely be the leaders of tomorrow—those students who are above average in ability, sometimes dramatically so, and who need levels of challenge not found in our current school curriculums. These highly able children should have opportunities to learn to think effectively, encounter a variety of people and ideas, benefit from individual pacing of learning experiences, and talk with intellectual peers (Halsted, 2009). It is up to our teachers, with support from parents and administrators, to provide these things for them, thus giving them the benefits of an appropriately challenging and intellectually stimulating school experience.

Chapter 1

Understanding Gifted Readers
in Middle School

> *Past inattention to teaching gifted students may in part be due to the problems of defining, identifying, and determining the characteristics of the gifted child.*
>
> ~William Durr

🖉 Chapter Highlights

- ➤ Who gifted readers are, and what problems they face
- ➤ The problems also faced by the adults who parent or teach these students
- ➤ Why it's important to focus on gifted readers in middle school
- ➤ How trade books can help
- ➤ How adults can help teens with perfectionism and underachievement

🖉 Research Connections

- ➤ T. M. Buescher & S. Higham (1985), *Helping Adolescents Adjust to Giftedness*
- ➤ J. W. Halsted (2009), *Some of My Best Friends Are Books* (3rd Edition)
- ➤ National Association for Gifted Children (2010), *Redefining Giftedness for a New Century: Shifting the Paradigm*
- ➤ S. Rakow (2005), *Educating Gifted Students in Middle School*
- ➤ S. B. Rimm (2008), *Why Bright Kids Get Poor Grades and What You Can Do about It*
- ➤ E. Ross & J. Wright (1985), *Teaching Strategies to Fit the Learning Styles of Gifted Readers in Middle School*
- ➤ J. T. Webb, J. L. Gore, E. R. Amend, & A. R. DeVries (2007), *A Parent's Guide to Gifted Children*

➤ C. S. Whitney, with G. Hirsch (2007), *A Love for Learning: Motivation and the Gifted Child*

➤ J. A. Willis (2009), *Inspiring Middle School Minds: Gifted, Creative, and Challenging*

Gifted adolescents face a variety of challenges when they enter middle school. In addition to the usual emotional turmoil that children face as they enter their teenage years, these bright, sensitive young people often find their experiences in middle school frustrating as they struggle through classes that lack challenge and provide few opportunities to grow academically. How do we as educators offer challenge? What will help us to understand these students and their needs?

Who Are Gifted Adolescents?

There are many definitions of what constitutes "gifted" and "talented." In 2010, the National Association of Gifted Children (NAGC) defined gifted students as follows:

> *Gifted individuals are those who demonstrate outstanding levels of aptitude (defined as an exceptional ability to reason and learn) or competence (documented performance or achievement in top 10% or rarer) in one or more domains. Domains include any structured area of activity with its own symbol system (e.g., mathematics, music, language) and/or set of sensorimotor skills (e.g., painting, dance, sports).*
>
> *The development of ability or talent is a lifelong process. It can be evident in young children as exceptional performance on tests and/or other measures of ability or as a rapid rate of learning, compared to other students of the same age, or in actual achievement in a domain. As individuals mature through childhood to adolescence, however, achievement and high levels of motivation in the domain become the primary characteristics of their giftedness. Various factors can either enhance or inhibit the development and expression of abilities.*

This definition (which can be found on www.nagc.org) provides a comprehensive look at giftedness. It refers to giftedness at all ages and in all areas. It also discusses evidence of high achievement and motivation, while also mentioning that the expression of these traits may be inhibited by certain factors.

While this definition is thorough and seemingly clear, gifted students are not always easy to identify. Some educators think that gifted children must demonstrate high ability in all areas, but it is important to note that it is possible for children to be gifted in only one or two areas and not in others. A child might be gifted in language arts but not in math, for example. Thus, educators may fail to identify students whose ability or aptitude test scores are averaged, without paying attention to the specific subject-area scores. Problems with identification also occur when students choose not to show their giftedness because they are shy or because of pressure to fit in with their peers in school. To them, it may be more important to belong to a particular group of peers or to stay in the background than to excel. This is especially prevalent among students who were identified as gifted in elementary school but who stop demonstrating their giftedness in middle school. Additional identification hurdles include problems with English not being a student's first language, which can clearly create a handicap when verbally-based tests are used to screen, as well as certain learning disorders or disabilities that students may have, despite their giftedness. In cases like these, teachers need to find ways that allow their students to showcase their gifts in other ways.

There are, unfortunately, many myths and misconceptions about gifted learners. Many educators believe that gifted children will "make it on their own" because of their advanced abilities. Educational resources need to be directed toward the children who are struggling, right? Not so fast! Just because students have the ability to process information quickly does not mean that they know how to access that information, what to do with that information, or how to build on that information. It also doesn't mean that they are emotionally ready to learn things that they may be intellectually ready to read about and study. The reality is that gifted students need teachers who will support and direct them, and especially who will be their advocates. When it comes to gifted readers, these students need teachers who will start with facts about their reading ability scores and then take a close look at the existing English program to see whether it will meet these students' language arts education needs.

Gifted Readers Speak Up

From their high intellect and their varying vantage points, middle school gifted readers bring different perspectives of self and culture into classrooms. Here, based on a survey I conducted a few years ago (Masiello, 2007), some gifted readers in middle school speak about their experiences:

➤ *Why do I have to read a book with my class when I've already read the book? My teacher won't let me read books that aren't on the seventh-grade book list because other grades might be using the book I want to read.* ~seventh-grade student

➤ *I don't enjoy reading since I entered middle school. When I was in elementary school, I was able to read every day. Now that I'm in sixth grade, I don't get to read books or novels; we only read worksheets that have stories and questions.* ~sixth-grade student

➤ *I don't want any of my friends to know I'm gifted in reading because they'd make fun of me. So now I act like I don't know the answers, and I try not to raise my hand and ask questions. But I feel like I'm not learning anything new, and it makes me so frustrated. I feel like I'm stuck and can't be myself. I feel confused.* ~eighth-grade student

➤ *My mom and dad keep pushing me to read, read, and read. I don't read in English class, and I don't have time in math, science, and geography. I don't want to disappoint my parents, but I just do not have time to read while in school.* ~sixth-grade student

➤ *Reading was easier for me in elementary school. I would like to read a book that interests me and then talk about it with my friends in class. Sometimes I learn more from my friends than from my teacher.* ~eighth-grade student

➤ *My teacher gave me a different book than what she gave to the rest of the class. My book had bad words in it and talked about issues dealing with sex. Then my teacher asked us to present our books to the class. I didn't want to because I was embarrassed to talk about the book in front of the class. I also didn't want to tell my parents because then they would talk to the teacher and I would be even more embarrassed.* ~seventh-grade student

Many issues, of course, may arise in the education of adolescent gifted readers. This book offers strategies that will allow caring adults to work through these issues with the gifted students they know who may be struggling or frustrated.

Teachers, Parents, and Administrators Speak Up

Several individuals share responsibility for the education of our middle schoolers. Teachers have the challenge of meeting their needs while in school; parents have the task of providing support, as well as providing a strong and healthy learning environment in the home; administrators must be involved because teachers and parents expect support and guidance from the school leaders.

Teachers Speak Up

Gifted students in middle school possess a variety of needs that sometimes cause confusion for those involved in their education. Reports on English classes and reading environments in middle schools indicate that teachers may not have the necessary tools to effectively teach reading to gifted adolescents. Some teachers report that their expertise is in math or science, and yet due to scheduling issues, they have been asked to teach language arts classes. It is important for these educators to learn instructional methods that will meet the needs of their gifted readers.

One particularly frustrating challenge facing teachers of gifted middle school readers is the structure of the typical middle school English curriculum. Historically, middle school teachers in content areas depended on elementary teachers to teach reading and comprehension skills. Today, middle school educators are recognizing that teaching reading is the responsibility of all teachers, regardless of their content specialty. Many middle school teachers admit that they don't have the training to teach reading, which leads some to the conclusion that they shouldn't have to. Fortunately, as administrators realize that all teachers in all subject areas should teach both reading and writing, and as attitudes change, professional development is now widely accepted as a way for teachers to receive the necessary training.

This change in the direction of the middle school English curriculum has prompted more staff development opportunities, which in turn have given classroom teachers more reading strategies. Many teachers, including math, science, and social studies teachers, have integrated these strategies into their classrooms, while others still struggle with issues related to teaching middle school gifted readers. Here are some of their questions and concerns:

➤ *How can I continue meeting the needs of gifted readers when I have so many diverse populations in my classroom?* ~sixth-grade teacher

➤ *What should I do when parents request that their gifted children read books that are challenging but not appropriate for their age?* ~seventh-grade teacher

➤ *How should I respond to my regular students when they ask why their friends are getting to read different books?* ~sixth-grade teacher

➤ *What if a child was identified as being gifted in reading in elementary school, but I am not seeing those same gifted characteristics in my classroom? How should I handle this situation with the student and with the parents? ~sixth-grade teacher*

➤ *How should I approach the issue of grades with gifted readers? The issues of grades and assessment are huge at my school. If my gifted readers receive a "B" on their vocabulary test because their word list was more challenging, then their parents request that they not participate in my enrichment groups. ~eighth-grade teacher*

➤ *Our school does not have a specific reading program. We have an English class that attempts to integrate reading into the curriculum, but this rarely happens. Because of state requirements, our English teachers focus on isolated skills, rather than reading appropriately selected literature. ~seventh-grade teacher*

Answers to all of these questions can be found within the pages of this text. Many of these teachers' concerns can be addressed with advice on how to communicate effectively—with students and parents alike (see Chapter 6). Assessment methods (Chapter 7), ways in which to differentiate instruction for gifted students (Chapter 3), and understanding problems like underachievement and perfectionism, which are so common in gifted teens (Chapter 1), are all included in this book, with suggestions and techniques that can be quite helpful for educators.

Parents Speak Up

Parents of middle school gifted readers often find it difficult to deal with school-related issues. They are concerned about their children's socialization and about teachers stereotyping their children. They also worry that their children are being assigned too much homework. They want optimal educational experiences that will help to motivate their children (Osborne, 2001), but they find it hard to advocate for a variety of reasons. They may fear becoming "the parent that everyone talks about in the teachers' lounge."

These parents ask their children questions about friends, teachers, and instruction. However, because their children may not always be willing to share information about their school experiences, it is difficult for the parents to know what is really going on in classrooms or how they might help make things more interesting, challenging, and enjoyable. Here are some of their comments:

➤ *When my son was in elementary school, he always came home and talked for hours about his day. Now that he's in middle school, he doesn't do this anymore. What happened to my "chatter-box"? I would like him to tell me about school and his friends. Is this typical of gifted adolescents? ~parent of a seventh-grade student*

➤ *My daughter's English teacher said the following on Back-to-School Night: "Don't expect a great deal of progress to be made this year. We have set up our curriculum so that we can address weaknesses in test-taking strategies and comprehension areas so that students will score higher on the mandated tests. If you are a parent of a gifted reader, you shouldn't worry. These students will succeed without my help. They will read on their own." My husband looked at me and told me to close my mouth. We both stared blankly ahead as the teacher continued. I quietly left the room. How can I approach this teacher about my concerns? Should I first speak to other parents so that I might understand this theory a bit better? ~parent of an eighth-grade student*

➤ *My son is an advanced reader who has lost his ambition to read. He doesn't seem unhappy by the fact that his bookshelf gets very little action these days. I have also noticed that his grades in English are slipping. Is my gifted reader unmotivated or simply underachieving for some hidden reason? ~parent of a sixth-grade student*

➤ *After another unproductive meeting with my son's English teacher, I decided to make an appointment to visit the principal. I left the meeting feeling satisfied because the principal was willing to listen to my concerns. But I was also disappointed with his reasoning for why reading is not a priority at his school. I was told that my son's English teacher is actually a math teacher who was recently asked to teach English. She has very little training related to gifted readers and lacks the strategies that some of the other teachers might possess. The principal said that he did not like or support the situation but had no other choices at this time. ~parent of an eighth-grade student*

Sometimes parents worry about problems with their child, sometimes with the teachers, and sometimes with the entire school environment. Information about the common characteristics and traits of gifted children, which can be found later in this chapter, is often reassuring and helpful. In addition, parents need to learn how to effectively communicate with school personnel (Chapter 6 in this text) in order to advocate for their child's learning needs. If the situation is distressing enough, parents can sometimes request a teacher change (using the appropriate chain of command—first meeting with the teacher, then the department head, then the principal), but depending on school policy, administrators are not always able to comply.

Parents should learn about program options for gifted students. An Internet search of books and resources for advocacy will provide a selection of titles that can be very helpful. Parents also often benefit from talking with teachers or the school guidance counselor about other academic options for their gifted child, such as independent study in an area that interests the child or an online course. In some instances, if administrators are supportive, a middle school student who is qualified can take a higher-level course—even a high school course—and earn early high school credit. School counselors and gifted program coordinators can help facilitate options like these.

Administrators Speak Up

While most of us agree that middle school teachers are challenged with meeting the needs of a diverse population of learners, few realize the pressures often faced by middle school administrators as well. These leaders admit that finding ways to provide staff, students, and parents with appropriate resources is a daunting task.

➤ *A parent knocked on my door and asked if she could have a few minutes of my time. Keeping the "open-door policy," I invited her into my office. Her concern was regarding her seventh-grade gifted son. His teacher was differentiating math instruction by simply giving the gifted students more math problems to complete. I had to assure this parent that I would look into the situation and that the school's philosophy for differentiation does not mean simply giving students more work.*

> ➤ *Our faculty meetings allow staff members to express themselves, whether the comment is positive or negative. Often, teachers note their concerns about not being adequately trained to teach specific subjects. This lack of training leads to a lack of confidence and a lack of communication with parents and students.*

> ➤ *Funding continues to be a heated topic of discussion in our school district. When it's time to discuss the budget, we find that the gifted program typically gets cut first. As an administrator, it becomes hard to maintain an effective gifted and talented program with cuts to the budget.*

These comments show just how important it is for administrators to understand the characteristics and needs of gifted students—and how they impact the work that our teachers do. Again, communication is key, with both teachers and parents. Teachers need opportunities to learn how to effectively differentiate instruction for their gifted students; Chapter 3 in this text can help. They can also learn from each other. Administrators might ask those teachers who feel comfortable doing so to share and discuss strategies that are working well in their classrooms with colleagues in the next faculty meeting. After a few months of idea sharing, teachers will begin filling their toolboxes with additional ideas that will help differentiate instruction.

When funds are tight, administrators need to become creative in finding ways to be flexible using the teachers and resources they already have. Perhaps they could do some cross-age grouping or single-subject acceleration for certain students, or allow some students to work with contracts on independent studies, which cost little or nothing but do require teacher support and monitoring.

Why Focus on Gifted Readers in Middle School?

In 2005, the National Center for Education Statistics published study results indicating that nationwide, students' reading scores and study skills tend to decrease in grades 6-8 (Perie, Grigg, & Donahue, 2005). Drs. Leo Fay, Jack Humphrey, and Carl Smith (2006) suggest that the decline in reading performance may be related to differences in middle school structure, as middle schools have supplanted junior high schools in recent decades. They ask, "Has the formation of middle schools to replace junior high schools three decades ago altered our thinking about learning development and subsequently shifted instructional energies in grades 6-8?" (p. 19).

In looking at why reading scores slide downward during the middle school years, Fay, Humphrey, and Smith note that when middle schools were originally restructured to provide more time in certain subject areas, reading classes and reading teachers were eliminated. This change provided more time for advisors to meet with students on a regular basis and for foreign language programs to be integrated into the middle school schedule. Policy makers felt that English teachers could combine teaching reading with teaching oral and written communication skills. However, this generally has not happened. But it is a trend that can be reversed.

Fortunately, as stated previously, professional development opportunities are now more readily available for educators who want to learn the best ways to teach their students about language and literature, as well as reinforce reading skills in all subject areas.

For those teachers who want to reach out to the most capable students in their classes, it is imperative that they also understand the characteristics and needs of gifted readers.

> *The middle school years can be challenging for gifted learners. A familiar marker of adolescents is the cognitive concept of the personal fable—the part of adolescent egocentrism involving an adolescent's sense of uniqueness.*
> ~ John W. Santrock

Characteristics of Gifted Readers

Many gifted middle school students express strong feelings of being misunderstood—by both classmates and teachers alike. These feelings sometimes originate in the elementary years, but by middle school, they can become overwhelming. Where once they were proud to be the first child with a correct answer, gifted students in the pre-teen and teenage years often find that they are teased and socially excluded for such behaviors. Hormonal changes leave them even more frustrated and confused, and many feel a desperate need to fit in with friends and classmates and to find social acceptance in whatever ways they can.

Educators know that this time period is a tumultuous one for students socially and emotionally, but it is even more difficult for students who are already different from the norm because of an exceptionality like giftedness. Teachers often cannot understand these students because the students do not understand themselves—they are so often complex and full of intensities and sensitivities, which seem strange to those unfamiliar with characteristics of giftedness. It becomes especially important for teachers to get to know their gifted students on an individual level; understanding how to react and respond to them may be difficult at first, but it is imperative. Gifted students—who often feel different and awkward—respond well to teachers who show an interest in them. Simple acceptance goes a long way toward building positive relationships and meeting these adolescents' needs.

Gifted students read for many different reasons. They may read for joy, or because they are told to do so, or to escape their everyday realities, or because certain books help them cope with issues they are facing in an environment that does not understand them. Although gifted readers are often self-motivated, they sometimes "shut down" if their fundamental needs are not being met. These needs include interesting, challenging, and meaningful reading material. If middle school teachers do not provide intellectual challenge as well as social and emotional support in their reading programs, they run a real risk of "losing" this population of students.

In her book *Some of My Best Friends Are Books* (3rd Edition, 2009), Judith Halsted—librarian, gifted education facilitator, and author—offers ideas for parents and teachers who want to use books and reading to help support the needs of their gifted readers. Her book (for both parents and teachers) contains information about the intellectual and emotional development of gifted students, as well as an extensive, annotated bibliography of more than 300 trade books appropriate for readers in grades K-12. The books are indexed by author, title, and subject. With giftedness in mind, Halsted has chosen titles that feature complex characters and themes, including many of the social and emotional issues that accompany giftedness, such as perfectionism, moral judgment, idealism, and feeling different.

In *Some of My Best Friends*, Halsted insists that:

> *Merely providing books is not enough, however. Knowledge of gifted children, discussion techniques, and children's literature will maximize the benefits that books offer. By filling the gaps in their knowledge, parents, teachers, counselors, and librarians can bring gifted children and books together more effectively. In so doing, they can help gifted children be themselves—comfortable in their present world and poised to grow into happy, productive adults.* (p. 7)

Thus, to adequately meet the needs of gifted students at the middle school level, and to help in selecting trade books for them to read, educators should have an understanding of the characteristics and needs of gifted children and youth.

Elinor Ross and Jill Wright (1985) agree, emphasizing that "Before working with middle school gifted students, the teacher should be aware of the characteristics and learning style preferences of these students" (p. 1). Fortunately, gifted readers in grades 6-8 often exhibit very noticeable characteristics, if adults know what to look for. Experts like Halsted (2009), David Levande (1999), and Mary Codd (1999) have created lists of some of these characteristics. Combining these different lists, we can say that gifted readers:

➤ Read avidly and absorb books well beyond their years
➤ Read a greater variety of literature, usually above grade level
➤ Have the desire to read both fiction and nonfiction
➤ Select their reading material purposefully and usually enjoy challenging books
➤ Understand language subtleties, as well as use language for humor
➤ Use words easily and accurately
➤ Have large, advanced vocabularies
➤ Often use their advanced vocabularies in new and innovative contexts
➤ Learn quickly and easily retain what is learned, thus requiring less drill and practice
➤ Show persistent, intellectual curiosity while asking questions
➤ Have a wide range of interests, which they like to explore in considerable depth

Ross and Wright (1985) add to this list by noting that many gifted readers tackle decision making sooner and begin to think in abstract ways earlier than their peers. When classroom teachers notice these behaviors in students, they should consider having the students tested for possible placement in the gifted program, if they are not already formally identified. Teachers should also be prepared to provide more challenging reading selections.

> *Although gifted adolescents go through the same developmental stages as their peers, they handle changes and transitions differently.*
> ~Felicia A. Dixon

Characteristics Have Pros and Cons

The previous list of characteristics of gifted students may lead adults to believe that positive traits for gifted readers only facilitate positive results. This is dangerous thinking. Several of the characteristics listed above need further investigation, because they can have both positive and negative consequences. For example, while curiosity is a good trait to have, and a curious child usually loves to learn about things, a highly curious gifted child can annoy others with her persistent questions, and fellow students may reject such a child socially. In addition, this child may disrupt class with her constant questioning, and teachers may find themselves irritated and off-topic because of her curiosity. This type of gifted child needs plenty of encouragement to keep on being curious, as well as an understanding adult to furnish answers, but she also may need some gentle guidance to pay attention to others' reactions and know when to stop.

Thomas Buescher and Sharon Higham (1985) report that gifted students between the ages of 11 and 15 often possess a range of problems as a result of their giftedness, such as perfectionism, competitiveness, unrealistic appraisal of their gifts, rejection from peers, confusion due to mixed messages about their talents, and parental and social pressures to achieve, as well as problems with school programs. All of these are common in middle school gifted students. When educators recognize and understand that these issues often go along with being gifted, they can begin to help these students.

One way to help is for teachers to select reading books in which characters in the book experience some of the same issues as those the students are experiencing. Integrating trade books into classrooms with gifted readers helps to meet these students' individual needs in many ways. If a character in a book experiences what the student is experiencing, the student can gain an understanding that he is not the only one in the world who has ever felt the way that he feels or dealt with the problems he is facing. As a bonus, he may gain some insight from the way in which the character handles situations in the book.

In an indirect way, showing gifted teens that they are not alone in their thoughts and feelings is a way of helping them become comfortable with their giftedness. Children begin to develop a self-concept and an identity during these middle school and teen years; reading about others who may have similar issues with intensities or moral concerns helps them feel less isolated and alone. Buescher and Higham (1985) note that this is important—children need to be able to accept themselves for who they are—and it may require intervention from teachers, administrators, parents, and counselors to help them accept their own unique set of strengths and weaknesses. Intervention should be fair and accurate because adolescents are often very sensitive to criticism, suggestions, and emotional appeals from others. Sometimes just listening to the student describe a dilemma is the best "intervention." Students don't necessarily want advice, but they do want acceptance and to know that adults care. Instead of suggestions on how the adolescent can deal with a situation, a better response might be: "Goodness, it sounds like this situation is upsetting to you. What are you considering as a way to respond?" This lets the student know you care, but that you have confidence that he can solve the problem himself.

Parents, friends, siblings, and even teachers often want to add their own expectations and observations to even the most advanced students' goals and aspirations. Buescher and Higham (1985) suggest that other people's expectations for the gifted are often problematic because they may differ from or compete with the child's own dreams and plans.

As Jim Delisle (1985) said, the "pull" of an adolescent's own expectations must swim against the strong current posed by the "push" of others' desires and demands. This "pulling" and "pushing" causes emotional and social turmoil among gifted adolescents, which can present as underachievement or perfectionism. Gifted adolescents need resources to help them adjust to their giftedness, as well as to communicate their own needs and desires.

Intellectual Development

Gifted education programming in local schools varies dramatically, leaving many families frustrated in their search for the best schools for their children. The path is not smooth for our gifted students, especially those whose interests are academic or intellectual. This is ironic, given that educational institutions should be the one place in which gifted children and young adults feel most at home. But gifted students possess intellectual needs that demand some extra attention in our classrooms, and this is where the problems begin.

There are many obstacles that can hinder intellectual development among the gifted population. These include economic barriers and social conditions, certain trends in education, and how well parents are able to help their children in their learning.

Reading promotes the acquisition of knowledge in many subject areas. Reading and interacting with books and other resources found in the home or in the public library help to build intellectual development. Children who are exposed to a variety of books and other enriching experiences at home, starting at a young age, are more likely to read books later in life. When reading and enrichment resources are limited due to parents' limited resources, children's intellectual development can be limited or handicapped as well.

Trends in education can also impede intellectual development. School systems experiencing budget cuts are often faced with the disturbing task of deciding which programs to fund and which ones to cut. Often, schools choose to minimize or eliminate specialized programs and will place students in larger instructional groups. This can hinder teachers' abilities to differentiate classroom experiences, which in turn affects many students—those who are non-English speaking, those who have learning disabilities, and those who are considered gifted and talented.

Parents vary greatly in their ability to help their children learn how to learn. Perhaps the parents have limited educational backgrounds themselves, they are struggling financially, or they are feeling overwhelmed by the powerful lure of electronic media, such as television, movies, video and computer games, etc. These differences make it even more urgent for teachers to try to reach out to help parents of middle school students stay involved in their children's education.

Social and Emotional Development

Meeting the intellectual needs of gifted students is one responsibility for educators, but it is equally or perhaps even more important to address these students' social and emotional needs. In recent years, both educators and parents have become more aware of how critically necessary it is to nurture the social and emotional development of gifted children, in addition to meeting their academic needs (Webb, Gore, Amend, & DeVries, 2007).

Gifted adolescents are unique in numerous ways; many exhibit issues with their intensity that contribute to feelings of not fitting in with their age peers. Because gifted adolescents are passionate about a variety of issues, they often get teased or criticized by their peers. Negative reactions from peers may then influence gifted adolescents to "go camouflage," as they are forced to choose between using their abilities or feeling accepted by their friends.

To further understand some of the social and emotional concerns of gifted adolescents, read some of these students' own responses to a survey administered in several different middle schools (Masiello, 2007):

> ➤ *I often feel that I have no friends. I see girls hanging out together and I want to be a part of their group.* ~sixth-grade female

> ➤ *When I get teased for being the "smartest kid in the class," I feel like I should not do well on the next test. That way I'll fit in and the other kids will stop teasing me.* ~eighth-grade male

> ➤ *I got a bad grade—well, actually, it was a C on a science test—and the other students laughed and said, "How does it feel to not always get A's on everything?" It made me want to crawl under my chair.* ~seventh-grade female

> ➤ *The kids in my class are always talking about doing things after school, but they never include me. I feel like everyone is looking at me or they feel bad for me because they know I'm not included.* ~seventh-grade male

> ➤ *I like to pretend that I can't read well or like I'm not interested in reading. This makes the other kids think I'm "cool" because I'm not trying to be the smart one in the class. But when I do this, I feel guilty and know my parents would be upset with me. Then I get all confused and don't really know how to feel or act.* ~eighth-grade female

Judith Halsted (2009) has identified many of the social and emotional issues that gifted children and young adults face. Most of these items reflect the emotional concerns expressed in the students' comments above:

> ➤ Feelings of isolation and rejection
> ➤ Feeling different from peers
> ➤ Downplaying abilities to fit in with age peers
> ➤ Displaying arrogance as a defensive behavior against rejection
> ➤ Withdrawing from social situations
> ➤ Exhibiting a lack of social skills
> ➤ Having trouble finding friends who understand and appreciate them
> ➤ Feeling misunderstood
> ➤ Difficulty getting along with others
> ➤ Reluctance to take risks
> ➤ Perfectionism
> ➤ Demonstrating inconsistent behaviors

As adolescents experience feelings of being different or alone, they look to adults for guidance. Teachers can use books to help address some of the social and emotional needs common to gifted students, as well as some of the concerns of specific students. Reading carefully selected trade books can help these students understand and accept their feelings and emotions. In addition, understanding and discussing the themes in these books can help gifted students learn to become valuable, contributing members in peer groups. The middle school years can thus be rewarding as well as challenging for gifted students.

Perfectionism

One of the most common problems that gifted adolescents experience is perfectionism. The need to perform at a high level or be "close to perfect" is a major characteristic associated with middle school students identified as gifted and talented (Siegle & Schuler, 2000). Students who exhibit signs of perfectionism typically set high and sometimes rigid standards for their work and are seldom satisfied, believing they should be able to do better.

These feelings develop for a variety of reasons. Sometimes parents set high standards and lofty goals for their children without realizing the possible consequences when these standards and goals are transmitted to gifted adolescents. Even good-natured banter can cause tension for sensitive teens. Teachers also inadvertently place pressure on gifted students in middle school because of these students' advanced abilities. They may expect their bright students to always do well on everything, and they may even express disappointment for less-than perfect grades from these students. And finally, the teens themselves can be the culprits of their problems with perfectionism. They often have succeeded in school without effort, attaining a school record of perfect grades. They may come to believe that everything they do should be perfect, and they may redo assignments or projects many times in an effort to maintain that perfect record. In fact, they may even avoid difficult classes or begin refusing to turn in work that is less than perfect, preferring to "fail by omission" rather than see evidence of an average performance, if they become too caught up in this phenomenon.

Some perfectionism is healthy, in the sense that students should strive to do their best. But extreme perfectionism can lead to problems. Understanding how perfectionism affects gifted adolescents is critical, because unhealthy perfectionism has been linked to anxiety, stress, and depression among this population of students. In fact, one of the most significant characteristics of gifted adolescents that may be associated with exposure to social and emotional disturbances is perfectionism (Delisle, 1991).

It is important for both parents and teachers to guide gifted adolescents so that they learn to develop healthy and reachable goals. Adults can help foster healthy habits and attitudes relating to perfectionism in various ways. One way that utilizes reading is to select a trade book in which the main character is struggling with perfectionism. The parent or teacher should read the book before recommending it to the child. Then, during or after reading, the parent or teacher can discuss events and themes in the book with the student, including how the main character deals with perfectionism. If the adult can gather together a small group of students and have them all read the book at the same time, these students can then share their thoughts with one another. "Individual or group discussion can lead to fresh insights that will help the child cope with difficult situations in her own life" (Halsted, 2009, p. 104).

One of the books that Halsted (2009) recommends for discussing perfectionism is *The Midwife's Apprentice* by Karen Cushman. This is the story of a young girl's "coming of age," and it was selected for inclusion here in this text (in Chapter 4) as one of the sample trade books to use with gifted adolescent readers.

Underachievement

Some gifted students go through a phase of underachievement as they progress through middle school. When a gifted student shows signs of not performing, teachers should respond by investigating why this is happening and learning ways in which to help. The following list consists of signs of underachievement that parents and teachers can watch for in their adolescent middle schoolers (Grobman, 2006):

➤ Declining grades
➤ Unfinished or missing schoolwork
➤ Disorganization
➤ Disinterest in school
➤ Making excuses or blaming others for problems
➤ Spending an excessive amount of time socializing, or the opposite—spending too much time alone

If adults recognize any of these signs, they can begin searching for more information. Understanding reasons for underachievement will lead to possible solutions that may help the gifted student begin achieving again in school. Sally Reis and Besty McCoach (2000) state that underachievement may be a result of:

➤ Insufficient challenge to spark the student's interest
➤ A lack of opportunities for the student to be creative
➤ Too much competition; if the child fails, he or she can become discouraged
➤ Too little or too much structure in the classroom
➤ Conflicts with teachers
➤ A recent move to a more or less difficult school
➤ Problems in the home, such as divorce or serious illness of a family member
➤ Over-protective parents, who foster dependency
➤ Health problems of the student
➤ A more serious problem, such as an attention deficit disorder or emotional or psychological disturbances

Once problems are identified and possible causes established, it becomes easier to find solutions. In an effort to help gifted students who are underachieving, teachers should provide time for enrichment, as well as opportunities for creativity. One particularly effective strategy is for the teacher to find a topic in which the student is interested and build from there to try to achieve a transfer of motivation. For example, if the teacher can determine that an underachieving student has a passion for airplanes, then she can find a way to integrate that topic into the student's math and science lessons, discussing how these subjects are needed to calculate wingspan, lift and drag, aerodynamics, etc. History becomes interesting when this student learns about, for instance, the role of aircraft in WWII. The teacher can also find reading materials for this student that relate to airplanes, including both nonfiction and fiction books that have flying as a theme, such as Amelia Earhart's attempted circumnavigational flight, which has recently been made into a movie. This student may also become motivated to succeed in school if he is informed that if he wants to work with airplanes as a career in life, he will need an education that includes subjects that may not interest him much now. Sometimes having a goal to work toward is a very effective motivator.

Since underachievement is such a complex issue involving so many different potential causes, teachers and parents may want learn more about it. Three books that can be especially helpful are *A Love for Learning: Motivation and the Gifted Child* (2007), by Carol Strip Whitney with Gretchen Hirsch, *Why Bright Kids Get Poor Grades and What You Can Do about It* (2008), by Sylvia Rimm, and *Inspiring Middle School Minds: Gifted, Creative, and Challenging* (2009), by Judy Willis.

Conclusion

Middle school curriculum is inextricably intertwined with social and emotional issues for all students, but especially for those who are gifted. This makes differentiation even more necessary, but also even more of a challenge. The reading strategies described in this book can provide both intellectual and social-emotional support.

✐ Key Points

1. Gifted students must deal with the normal challenges that accompany adolescence, as well as additional issues that result from their exceptionalities.

2. Gifted teens often struggle with feelings of differentness and isolation from their age peers.

3. Teachers of gifted readers in middle school report not having appropriate resources to adequately teach these students.

4. Understanding the common characteristics associated with gifted readers can help teachers choose appropriate books for them to read.

5. Using books with gifted students in middle school can help them to see that they are not alone in their feelings.

6. Perfectionism is a trait that is common to many gifted students, but there are strategies that teachers can use to help perfectionistic students.

7. There are many ways teachers can support students who are considered gifted but who are underachieving in school.

Chapter 2

Using Books with Gifted Readers in Middle School

> *Quality literature involving gifted characters should be available to gifted children and adolescents to encourage reflection about their feelings, concerns, and interests. These books can help students gain insight into their own lives and identify with others.*
>
> ~Bertie Kingore

✎ Chapter Highlights

- ➤ Using trade books with middle school gifted readers
- ➤ How to choose books to use with gifted readers
- ➤ The benefits of bibliotherapy
- ➤ A suggested list of titles

✎ Research Connections

- ➤ N. K. Aiex (1993), *Bibliotherapy*
- ➤ N. Atwell (2007), *The Reading Zone: How to Help Kids Become Skilled, Passionate, Habitual, Critical Readers*
- ➤ J. W. Halsted (2009), *Some of My Best Friends Are Books* (3rd Edition)
- ➤ B. Kingore (2002), *Reading Strategies for Advanced Primary Readers*
- ➤ V. Monseau & G. Salvner (2000), *Reading Their World: The Young Adult Novel in the Classroom*

Reading Instruction in Middle School

To travel across the seas to a foreign land…to dive into the thoughts of a talented mind…to escape…to remember…to live a new life…to learn. Ahh! To open the cover of an interesting new book!

Reading curriculum in middle schools is typically integrated into the overall English program. While this sort of English curriculum works well for many students, it does not usually benefit students who are advanced readers. Books for gifted readers should be challenging, with plenty of complexity—of language, character, setting, and plot. Basal readers are often a mismatch with gifted readers.

Middle school classrooms usually contain several types of readers. Some students have difficulty reading, comprehending, and applying even basic information; other students are reading and comprehending at grade level; and still others are reading and comprehending two to three grade levels (or more) above their current grade placement. With such a wide span of ability levels in their classrooms, teachers find it very difficult to provide reading instruction that meets the needs of all learners.

What happens in many middle school language arts classrooms is that students who are gifted in reading are required to maintain the same instructional pace as the rest of the class. Everyone in the class reads the same book—usually part of a reading series adopted by the school system and which usually provides step-by-step directions as to how and when teachers introduce and teach certain skills. Teachers may appreciate that the planning is mostly done for them, but on the other hand, they are often frustrated with the limitations of these basal reading textbooks when it comes to the skills that they want to introduce in their classrooms. The reality is that with so many different levels of abilities to teach to—from learning disabled to advanced readers—it is simply impossible to meet the needs of all students with basal texts.

There are other problems with the use of adopted textbooks in heterogeneous classrooms. Let's take a closer look.

Using Adopted Textbooks for Reading Instruction

The reason that school systems endorse the use of a single basal text has to do with the federally mandated standardized tests which are required in the United States. Knowing that all students have received the same instruction in reading (instruction geared toward maximizing standardized test scores) provides school districts with a certain sense of security when their students take the tests. Educators know that all students have read the same content and have had the same or similar instruction. However, this practice becomes a major concern when it comes to planning curriculum for advanced readers.

Researchers have noted problems encountered by high-ability students when textbooks (basal readers) are the primary source for reading instruction. H.T. Bernstein (1985) elaborates:

> *Even if there were good rules of thumb about the touchy subject of*
> *textbook adoption, the issue becomes moot when a school district buys*
> *only one textbook, usually at a certain grade level, for all students in a*
> *subject or grade. Such a purchasing policy pressures adoption*

*committees to buy books that the least-able students can read. As a
result, the needs of more advanced students are sacrificed.* (p. 465)

Particular difficulties exist for students who read above grade level. Chall and Conrad (1991) describe studies that focused on gifted students who read two or more grade levels above their peers, concluding, "Their reading textbooks provided little or no challenge since they were matched to the students' grade placement, not reading levels" (p. 19). Middle school gifted readers themselves also expressed concerns about the lack of challenge provided for them in their English classrooms.

In another study of gifted readers in middle school, Taylor and Frye (1988) found that 78% to 88% of advanced students could easily pass pre-tests on comprehension skills before the information was covered in the reading textbook. In other words, these students were not actually learning the material presented to them; they had already mastered it and were instead simply "marking time." In short, basal reading texts lack appropriate challenge for gifted readers and are clearly not appropriate for such advanced students.

If Not Adopted Textbooks, Then What?

Educators at the secondary level should consider integrating appropriately selected trade books into their English and reading programs. Using high-quality literature with middle school readers is critical if we want to keep them motivated and progressing in their learning (Richards, 2008).

Teachers can reflect on the following list of questions as they begin their search for quality literature to meet specific student needs:

➤ Does the trade book contain challenging language and interesting literary techniques that will appeal to gifted readers?

➤ Is it appropriate in content for this age group of students?

➤ How can the book facilitate the teaching of basic English skills, including grammar and punctuation, without the use of worksheets and adopted textbooks?

➤ Can the integration of this or other trade books promote group discussions so that students can comfortably express their thoughts and feelings?

➤ How can reading this book help students who are struggling with social and emotional issues?

Using Trade Books in the Classroom

Teachers who use trade books have many options when working with gifted readers in mixed-ability classrooms (Richards, 2008). The simplest choice is for teachers to select titles that will appeal to students at nearly any ability level so that all of the students can read the same book. Then, instead of differentiating by assigning different books, the activities involving the book can be differentiated based on student ability levels. Teachers can arrange students into three or four different groups, according to their degree of ability, and ask them to provide answers to questions that relate to the book—questions that increase in difficulty for the more advanced students. While one group is answering questions based on comprehension, another group might be providing answers that require analysis or synthesis of ideas or events in the book.

Alternatively, teachers may want to select different titles for different groups of students. These teachers can choose two or three books to read based on the differing reading abilities of their students. Each group should read a book that stretches the students academically but is not so difficult that it is frustrating to them.

Teachers using trade books during reading instruction can also allow students to choose titles based on the students' individual interests. Of course, the teacher should have final approval of any selection made by a student.

These last two options for differentiating reading instruction using trade books obviously require more work on the part of the educator, since he or she will need to create questions, form discussion topics, and plan activities relating to more than one title at a time. However, there are many resources available to help teachers with these tasks, including the ideas and activities in this book, and once they are used, these activities can be reused with other titles and other students in consecutive years.

Using trade books enables teachers to differentiate reading instruction in a variety of ways. By understanding strategies for differentiating reading, whether by reading activity, reading content, or student interest, teachers can meet the needs of students more effectively.

Using Well-Chosen Books

Gifted readers like books with complex themes and characters, as well as interesting and unusual settings and plots. They enjoy reading about people, places, and experiences that are new to them, including books about people from other countries and cultures, histories, and biographies. A challenging book is sometimes even more enjoyable if the student has an opportunity to discuss it with a friend, classroom peer, teacher, school counselor, parent, or some other adult who has also read the book.

A wonderful benefit of reading books with complex issues and themes is that gifted students—who are complex individuals themselves—are often able to notice and assimilate new ideas and concepts that may be useful to them. They not only gain new perspectives, but they may apply some of what they learn from reading books to their own lives. Perhaps they learn new ideas for improving friendships or family relationships, or maybe they learn about tolerance for others from the concept of "walking in someone else's shoes" (Hébert & Kent, 2000).

The goal is for adults to select books with enough interest that students are excited to read them and discuss what they've read. When parents and teachers select books that feature multiple, complex themes such as idealism, moral concerns, perfectionism, judgment, decision making, friendship, and aloneness—themes that may be issues in the students' own lives—students are able to grow intellectually, socially, and emotionally in these areas.

Bibliotherapy for Gifted Readers

The guided reading described above, in which students find connections within the literature to their own lives—and thus also ways in which to handle similar problems—is often called *bibliotherapy*. In bibliotherapy, readers identify with the characters and/or themes in a book; they notice how the characters react to pressures and events that occur in their lives, how they make decisions, how they grow and mature during the course of the book. When adolescents read books with themes that interest them and then discuss the books with one or more other individuals, they can learn invaluable lessons about human behavior and the potential for growth. As Nola Kortner Aiex (1993) states, "Bibliotherapy can be defined as the use of books to help people solve problems" (p. 1).

As noted earlier, gifted adolescents face a variety of social and emotional issues beyond what many average-ability teens face. These students may find solace and relief in books that depict characters who overcome similar problems. Teachers who are familiar with characters and themes in a variety of trade books will be able to select appropriate books for specific students. Aiex (1993) believes that parents and teachers who use bibliotherapy can help to:

> *…develop an individual's self-concept, increase an individual's understanding of human behavior and motivation, foster an individual's honest self-appraisal, provide a way for a person to find interests outside of self, relieve emotional or mental pressure, show an individual that he or she is not the first or only person to encounter such a problem, show an individual that there is more than one solution to a problem, help a person discuss a problem more freely and help an individual plan a constructive course of action to solve a problem.* (p. 4)

Classroom teachers, counselors, librarians, and parents all report success when using bibliotherapy with students. Although this type of reading works well in an individual format between one adult and one student, it is also an excellent strategy to use in reading programs for groups of advanced readers at the secondary level. A group discussion facilitates an atmosphere that allows gifted students to share with other students who may have had similar experiences. However, it is important to learn about techniques and guidelines for this strategy, because students may bring up sensitive issues. It is a good idea to develop and post rules for the group so that it is clear that students are expected to express respect for one another during the discussions and show consideration for privacy issues outside of the discussions. Well-prepared teachers can then establish open lines of communication as students read the books and examine topics. Edwards and Simpson (1986) suggest the following guidelines for using bibliotherapy:

➤ Select books with literary merit.

➤ Aim toward helping students with minor issues or questions. (Save the serious problems for trained professionals.)

➤ Select literature that contains content, characterizations, and situations that are real and believable.

➤ Provide for discussion time so that students can recall information and discuss higher-level concepts.

Aiex (1993) recommends a specific order of events when using bibliotherapy in classrooms:

> *The basic procedures in conducting bibliotherapy are: motivate the students with introductory activities, provide time for reading the material, allow incubation time, provide follow-up discussion time and use questions that will lead persons from literal recall of information through interpretation, application, analysis, synthesis, and evaluation of information.* (p. 1)

For bibliotherapy to be effective, educators and counselors must select well-written and appropriate books for their students. It is important to examine the content of any book before recommending it to middle school-age children. While some students might be capable of reading a given book, the content may not be appropriate for their age. Understanding the written words on a page helps students score well on tests that assess comprehension; however, adolescents may not yet have the maturity level to understand and appreciate intricacies of character, plot, and theme in some classic books. For example, reading and understanding the vocabulary in *Moby Dick* or *Doctor Zhivago* is different from relating personally to the themes of these books. Middle school students have not yet had enough life experience to fully understand and appreciate some of the deeper messages in some of the greatest works of literature. In the meantime, the field of young adult literature is growing, and there are challenging books written for this age group that are appropriate for their maturity level.

The key in guiding adolescent readers, then, is finding appropriate books at the appropriate time. A good book for talented readers should stretch them beyond what they've read before, but not so far above their knowledge and comprehension that they become frustrated with it. Those responsible for guiding adolescents' reading can usually get excellent suggestions for books from librarians, who have often taken courses specializing in adolescent literature and are trained to help with book selection. There are also annotated bibliographies that can help, such as Halsted's book *Some of My Best Friends Are Books* (3rd Edition, 2009).

Selecting Books for Gifted Readers

When selecting books to use in classrooms containing gifted readers, educators should become familiar with standard characteristics of appropriate literature. Halsted (2009) identifies certain types of books that appeal to and are typically appropriate for gifted readers. She recommends using books that (pp. 192-194):

➤ Make strong demands on the readers' vocabulary, with language that is on a high level

➤ Use complex sentence structure and advanced vocabulary; pronunciation guides, maps, and glossaries are especially helpful

➤ Possess language patterns and vocabularies typical not only of the present, but of other times and places as well

➤ Provide settings that evoke an experience of other lifestyles

➤ Present unresolved problems and compel the reader to draw some conclusions

Monseau and Salvner (2000) offer additional criteria for educators to consider. They suggest that books containing the following elements will most stimulate and challenge gifted young adults:

➤ Complex characters who seek to resolve conflicts with tremendous consequences to themselves and the world

➤ Vividly depicted minor characters

➤ Rich settings in fiction and nonfiction

➤ Skillful use of suspense and flashbacks

➤ Narratives told from various points of view

➤ Identifiable thematic issues that matter to teens and to everyone

Teachers must understand that choosing quality literature to use with gifted readers in middle school is critical. Bright students at this age find school bothersome if they feel that their time is being "wasted" on "busy work" that is beneath their academic ability. They may become bored, frustrated, or depressed. They may rebel and act out, perhaps with anger or sarcasm, or perhaps in more subtle ways, such as through underachievement. They wonder why they should put forth effort on lessons that hold no interest or value to them. When this happens, parents and teachers may be surprised to find their high-ability students attaining only mediocre grades. And because some of these students lack skills to communicate their feelings of frustration in appropriate ways, they may begin showing problem behaviors, such as treating others, including adults, with disrespect.

Many of these problems can be avoided if we simply give our gifted adolescent students appropriately challenging material to study, which includes trade books that offer interesting and yet demanding reading and which provide our young teens with opportunities to develop and use their higher-level thinking skills. The following two pages can be copied by educators and used to help select appropriate books for their students.

Reading Inventory, Grades 6-8

Name:		Date:

As your teacher, I feel it is important to learn about your reading needs so that I can create appropriate lesson plans to use in our classroom. Please think carefully as you provide your answers to the questions below.

Directions: *Please circle all that apply for the following questions.*

I enjoy reading:	at home.	at school.	everywhere.
I enjoy reading:	fiction.	nonfiction.	biographies.
	mysteries.	poetry.	anything I can get my hands on.
I prefer reading:	by myself.	in a group	with a friend.
If given a choice, I would:	like to talk about books with others.	not like to talk about books with others.	sometimes like to talk about books with others.
When given a reading assignment, I:	complete it immediately.	procrastinate and complete it at the last minute.	take my time and read it before the due date.
My reading experiences have been:	positive.	negative. (Please explain the negative experiences on the back of this sheet.)	I have had different experiences in different grades.

Please provide answers to the following questions:

1. My greatest strength in reading is: _____

2. One thing I need to improve about my reading is: _____

3. I want to read more books about: _____

4. One thing that frustrates me in English class is: _____

5. One thing I like in English class is: _____

6. Sometimes the English class makes me feel: _____

A Guide to Selecting Books for Gifted Readers in Middle School

This chart lists several titles that are appropriate for gifted middle school readers. Teachers looking for ways to meet the academic, social, and emotional needs of their gifted students will find these books helpful (Austin, 2003; Halsted, 2009; Kingore, 2002).

Title/Author of Book	Grade Levels	Elements and Characteristics
Go and Come Back Joan Abelove	7-10	Unusual perspective; offers various points of view; facilitates discussion about seeing others' views
Kids on Strike Susan Bartoleth	5-8	Portrayal of gifted role models; explores the idea of social responsibility
Aria of the Sea Dia Calhoun	5-8	Fantasy; gifted protagonists facing their own struggles
I Am the Cheese Robert Cormier	6-9	Challenging structure; rich plot that raises many questions
A Step from Heaven An Na	7-10	Imagistic language; depicts different cultures and diversity
The Music of Dolphins Karen Neese	6-8	Challenging content; includes ethical dilemmas, such as expressing opinions and making judgments
Buried Onions Gary Soto	6-9	Distinctive, metaphoric language; ambiguous ending
Welcome to the Ark Stephanie Tolan	5-8	Gifted protagonists; includes unusual narrative techniques
Act I, Act II, Act Normal Martha Weston	6-8	Depicts the emotional needs of a middle school character; promotes discussion about identity and differences

✏ Key Points

1. Most middle school classrooms contain students of widely varying ability levels, making it difficult for teachers to plan appropriate reading instruction for all students.

2. Adopted textbooks are often unchallenging for advanced readers in middle school; gifted students report a lack of challenge in their English programs.

3. Using trade books in place of adopted textbooks helps teachers focus on the needs of gifted readers.

4. Quality literature involving characters who struggle with the same issues as gifted adolescents should be available to advanced readers in middle school.

5. Bibliotherapy can be a very effective way of using books to help students solve problems.

6. Teachers should provide time for discussion of the books so that students can recall information and discuss concepts at higher levels.

7. Selecting books for gifted readers requires knowledge of appropriate, well-written literature with complex plots and themes, as well as interesting settings and characters.

Chapter 3
Differentiation Strategies for Gifted Readers

> *Books for the gifted need to be assessed not only in terms of language, structure, and content, but also by their potential for eliciting intellectual responses from the readers.*
>
> ~Barbara Baskin & Karen Harris

✎ Chapter Highlights
- ➤ What differentiation of instruction means
- ➤ Why gifted readers need differentiation in their reading programs
- ➤ Differentiation strategies to use before, during, and after reading

✎ Research Connections
- ➤ B. Clark (2008), *Growing Up Gifted: Developing the Potential of Children at Home and at School* (7th Edition)

- ➤ D. Heacox (2002), *Differentiating Instruction in the Regular Classroom: How to Reach and Teach All Learners Grades 3-12*

- ➤ K. B. Rogers (2002), *Re-Forming Gifted Education: How Parents and Teachers Can Match the Program to the Child*

- ➤ C. A. Strip (2000), *Helping Gifted Children Soar*

- ➤ C. Tomlinson (2001), *How to Differentiate Instruction in Mixed-Ability Classrooms*

- ➤ S. Winebrenner (2001), *Teaching Gifted Kids in the Regular Classroom*

Students who are more advanced in their reading and comprehension abilities than their classmates need to be exposed to more challenging—i.e., differentiated—instruction in reading. This chapter describes the steps necessary to begin the process of differentiation. There are many different methods and strategies that can be used to differentiate instruction—before, during, and after reading with gifted students—and these strategies can be used with *all* students because they are easy to adapt to any level.

My current position as a gifted and talented resource teacher allows me to visit various schools and to meet with many creative teachers who work at different grade levels. I often brainstorm with these teachers strategies that can be used to introduce or promote a book, extend learning after reading, and evaluate student understanding. The following sections will help you develop your own strategies.

What Is a Differentiated Classroom?

Differentiated classrooms are those that meet the needs of all learners. Both slow and rapid learners receive appropriate work and instruction based on their learning needs. Carol Tomlinson, a specialist in curriculum and gifted education, writes: "In a differentiated classroom, commonalities are acknowledged and built upon, and student differences become important elements in teaching and learning…" (2001, p. 5). According to Tomlinson (2001), differentiation (p. 12):

➤ Means "shaking up" what goes on in the classroom so that students have multiple options for taking in information

➤ Blends whole-class, group, and individual instruction

➤ Provides multiple approaches to content, process, and product

Diane Heacox (2002) adds to these points, saying that differentiation also means (p. 17):

➤ Recognizing the learning diversity represented in today's classrooms

➤ Acknowledging what students already know and can do

➤ Using flexible instructional grouping to provide opportunities for students to learn with others who have similar needs, styles, or preferences

In many classrooms, gifted students don't have a chance to progress because they have already mastered the skills or material that the other students are learning. If a teacher has not administered a pre-test or some other kind of survey of the students, she may not know which children have already mastered the material she plans to teach. Or, if she does know, she may not know what to provide for the advanced students beyond what the rest of the class is learning. Gifted students should have the opportunity to learn new skills and concepts that they haven't been exposed to previously. Without new learning, these students do not progress academically.

It is crucial for educators to manipulate the curriculum in ways that allow for gifted students to achieve academic growth. Susan Winebrenner (2001) emphasizes that these kinds of curriculum changes can provide consistent opportunities for gifted students to enjoy learning and be as challenged and productive as possible. "Differentiation means providing gifted students with different tasks and activities than their peers, tasks that lead to real learning for them" (p. 5). Carol Strip, author of *Helping Gifted Children Soar* (2000), concurs: "Differentiation for gifted students means providing learning options that meet the students' special needs for acceleration of content and greater depth, breadth, and complexity of instruction" (p. 71).

A few examples of differentiation for advanced readers may be helpful. If the class is reading Mark Twain's *Tom Sawyer* and the teacher wants to challenge some of the gifted students who have already read this book, she might talk with them in a small group and describe some other works by Twain that they might read instead, such as *Life on the Mississippi, The Prince and the Pauper,* or *A Connecticut Yankee in King Arthur's Court.* After reading one or more of these, a single student or a small group of students could discuss the book with the teacher, focusing on themes such as the recurring social criticism found in Twain's writings, as well as how Twain uses satire to express his anger. Delving deeper into an author's work and analyzing it is an example of greater depth and complexity of instruction.

As another example, say that students are studying drama and reading the play *West Side Story.* If some students complain that they already know this story from having seen the movie, the teacher could send a small group of advanced students to find an audio or video recording in the public library of Shakespeare's *Romeo and Juliet.* This group could listen to or view this work and then compare the plot to that of *West Side Story.* This is another example of offering gifted students greater depth and breadth of learning.

Here is a different example. Students who are gifted in language arts may be especially proficient at understanding the mechanics of writing. If the class is studying grammar, sentence construction, parts of speech, and correct noun/verb agreement, an alternate assignment that might be interesting and challenging for the students who have demonstrated a thorough understanding of these principles on a pre-test might be to copy one or two sentences from a paragraph written by an author recognized as an excellent writer, and then try writing their own sentences using that author's style. Authors and classic works from the library that would be good to use for this project include: Jack London (*The Call of the Wild*), Madeline L'Engle (*A Wrinkle in Time*), Astrid Lindgren (*Pippi Longstocking*), L.M. Montgomery (*Anne of Green Gables*), Phyllis Naylor (*Shiloh*), Armstrong Sperry (*Call It Courage*), Elizabeth Speare (*The Sign of the Beaver*), Stephanie Tolan (*A Time to Fly Free*), Sharon Creech (*Chasing Redbird*), Paul de Kruif (*Microbe Hunters*), Paula Danziger (*The Cat Ate My Gymsuit*), Irene Hunt (*Across Five Aprils*), Randall Jarrell (*The Bat-Poet*), Eric Kelly (*The Trumpeter of Krakow*), and Scott O'Dell (*My Name Is Not Angelica*). A benefit of this assignment is that students may become interested in reading the book!

Differentiation for Gifted Students

Teachers reading this may now be asking, "How can I do all of this while still meeting the rest of the curriculum requirements?" While I agree that beginning to differentiate instruction is time consuming, it does get easier as teachers and students realize they can work together. Students may have ideas for things they would like to study. In fact, teachers can ask the students for ideas of what they would like to learn or work on. Parents might also have ideas. Both parents and students are often pleased to be asked. Strip (2000) explains: "It's actually easy to engage gifted children because they are open to so many different approaches and are excited about opportunities to accelerate or expand their learning in certain interest areas" (p. 72).

Teachers should note that differentiated instruction must be qualitative instead of quantitative, meaning that gifted students should not simply be given "more of the same" kind of work to do (Rogers, 2002). For example, giving advanced students twice as many story problems to complete as their average-ability classmates is not differentiated instruction. Using the previous Mark Twain example, asking gifted students to do the same work, the same quizzes, and the same written assignments as the rest of the class in addition working with the other novel is not what differentiation means. Piling on extra work punishes students for being smart and completing their work quickly. What we want to do is offer them quality work that interests them and that helps them progress in their skills—in this instance, their language arts skills. Barbara Clark, author of the seminal textbook *Growing Up Gifted* (7th Edition, 2008), states that gifted students need educational programs that offer small-group discussions, flexibility, respect for other's ideas, time for reflection, and the opportunity to compare communication and decision-making processes with academic peers.

Differentiating Reading Instruction for Gifted Readers

If you are a teacher reading this, then you'll probably remember the anxiety you faced during the first week of school when you realized that your fifth-grade classroom contained some students who were reading on the second-grade level and others who were reading on the eighth-grade level. We've all been there!

At that point, though, you had to make a decision. Did you follow the basal reading text and keep everyone reading on the same level through the use of the same story? Or did you look for supplemental books, such as trade books, that could help you meet the needs of all of the students in the class? Even though it takes extra time and planning, the only fair choice is to locate more challenging materials for the students who need them. In fact, the lack of challenging materials is one factor that discourages the continued development of advanced readers (Kingore, 2002).

The first step in providing differentiated reading instruction is for teachers to carefully examine their current reading programs. They should consider the questions: *What specific skills do I need to teach all students? Which skills do I want each and every student to master?* Scrutinizing one's reading program in this way will help to ensure that all students meet criteria established by local school districts and that no learning gaps occur during differentiated instruction. Once educators have made a list of the fundamental skills that all of their students need to master, they will have a clear understanding of the basic needs of the classroom.

Next, teachers should understand the importance of assessment so that they have an accurate knowledge of the students' actual ability levels. Knowing student ability levels is critical as teachers select appropriate trade books and instructional strategies. Assessment must be ongoing as students progress in their learning and skills. Progress will be documented in portfolios, running records, standardized test scores, writing samples, anecdotal records, and rubrics. Information collected from these various evaluation tools is both important and useful when designing a differentiated classroom. Chapter 7 in this text contains detailed information on assessment.

The information that follows will help educators provide challenging materials for gifted readers through the use of differentiated reading strategies. Suggested activities invite the teacher to explore whole-group instruction, as well as small-group projects and individual, one-on-one time with the teacher. Carol Tomlinson (2001) states that "a differentiated classroom is marked by a repeated rhythm of whole-class preparation, review and sharing, followed by opportunity for individual or small-group exploration, sense-making, extension and production" (p. 3). The methods described below will help create the differentiated classroom that Tomlinson describes.

Ways to Differentiate Instruction for Gifted Readers

Permission to Read Ahead

This simple strategy gives rapid readers opportunities to read ahead of the group by completing a "Contract for Permission to Read Ahead" (Winebrenner, 2001). It allows gifted readers to remain challenged and motivated without telling anyone else in the class about the outcomes in the story. The teacher and the student must sign the contract to show that both are in agreement. The student then uses the extra time left over while the rest of the class is still reading to complete enrichment activities or higher-level thinking tasks related to the story.

Contract for Permission to Read Ahead

Directions: Please initial each statement to show that you agree with it. Then sign the contract.

_____ I *will not* tell anyone anything about the story until everyone has finished reading it.

_____ I *will not* participate in prediction activities.

_____ I *will* participate in the alternate activities and assessments.

Student's Signature: _____Date_____

Teacher's Signature: _____

Curriculum Compacting

Curriculum compacting is another way to differentiate instruction for gifted readers. When a teacher finds that certain students have already mastered a skill or set of material, he or she allows them to skip past that material, thus "compacting" their time with a given curriculum or set of assignments. Curriculum compacting can be used to make adjustments for students in any subject area and at any grade level. Sally Reis and Joseph Renzulli (2005) list the following steps to compact curriculum for students:

➤ Define the goals and outcomes of a particular unit or segment of instruction.

➤ Determine and document which students have already mastered most or all of a specified set of learning outcomes.

➤ Provide replacement strategies for material already mastered through the use of instructional options that enable a more challenging and productive use of the students' time.

Teachers who wish to use curriculum compacting for gifted readers often begin by administering a pre-test, usually from the basal text series. Students who show mastery by scoring 85% or better on the pre-test should receive alternative instruction for that part of the basal text curriculum. Teachers can then allow these students to read books selected either by the teacher or the students while the rest of the class works with the basal text. These alternate reading selections should "stretch" the students in some area that will ensure academic growth. Perhaps they are at a higher reading level with more difficult vocabulary, or maybe they have a complex plot. All students are thus reading at the same time, but advanced readers are reading material that is more appropriate for their academic needs.

Susan Winebrenner (2001) helps us visualize curriculum compacting by using the word "trash." She says that compacting helps students deal with the part of the curriculum that represents "trash" to them because they don't need it—they are finished with it, they have mastered it, and they can throw it away. After taking a pre-test and demonstrating an understanding of material about to be presented, students can spend their newly earned spare time working on enrichment opportunities.

Learning Contracts

When teachers compact the curriculum for their gifted students, these students are left with extra time to work on other activities and projects. One way for teachers to keep them busy with material that is both interesting to them and intellectually appropriate is through the use of learning contracts. Learning contracts give gifted readers opportunities to read, discuss, analyze, and write independently, using literature that they find challenging. The contracts list books and activities that the gifted readers will complete while the other students work with the basal text. Learning contracts can include assignments, extension activities, and criteria or timelines that the students must follow. Teachers can allow students to have some input as to the content of the contract. Both student and teacher then sign the learning contract to show that they are in agreement.

Learning contracts can be used with gifted students in many subject areas. The primary advantage of these contracts is that they customize learning to meet individual needs, thus allowing gifted students to take more ownership of their learning. Examples of learning contracts can be found in Susan Winebrenner's book *Teaching Gifted Kids in the Regular Classroom* (2001) and Carol Strip's book *Helping Gifted Children Soar* (2000).

Activity Menus

Activity menus are another tool that teachers can use when their gifted students are left with extra time to fill, either because the curriculum has been compacted for them or because they have finished their regular work early. Activity menus provide students with a variety of activities that extend a unit of study. Susan Winebrenner (2001) explains how teachers can use reading activity menus to facilitate choice, as well as to provide gifted readers with opportunities to take ownership of their learning. She advises teachers to prepare a list of activities from which students may choose, and then allow the students to work on one or more of those activities when their assigned work is finished. Alternatively, teachers can invite students to come up with their own ideas and projects, subject to teacher approval. Either way, the students must record their work in a daily log to show their progress.

Educators who choose to use activity menus with gifted readers can accommodate many different learning styles. For example, there may be activities listed on the menu which involve building dioramas or creating sculptures relating to the book that the students are reading; these particular activities will be of interest to students who learn best by working with their hands. Students who learn best by reading to locate facts will be able to choose these types of activities from the activity menu. Both students and teachers appreciate the simplicity and flexibility of this process.

A sample reading activity menu follows. These menus can be filled out by both the teacher and the student and can be put in the student's portfolio, which is a folder containing samples of the student's best work from the entire school year.

Reading Activity Menu

Student's Name:		Timeframe:
Teacher:		Grade: ___ Date:

Directions: *You may choose two of the activities listed below to do after your regular assignments are finished. Record the dates you work, as well as any notes you may have about the projects.*

Dates:

Activity:

_____ Create a new ending to the story.

_____ Find two other students who have read the story. Conduct an interview to find out how they liked the story. Take notes, and later write about the findings of the interview.

_____ Write a play or a puppet show that summarizes the story you read.

_____ Create a children's book that is similar to the story. Think about plot, setting, conflict, and so on. Illustrate your story.

You may also choose to create your own two activities to substitute for the ones above. Think about areas that interest you. Write your ideas below, and share them with your teacher.

_____

_____

_____

_____

Student comments:_____

_____

Teacher comments:_____

_____

Adapted from Winebrenner (2001)

Anchor Activities

Similar to activity menus, anchor activities can be used with all students, because the activities can be tailored to different ability levels, making them a favorite form of differentiation with teachers. In addition, they can be used with any subject, as well as with whole-group or small-group assignments.

Anchor activities are ongoing activities related to the subjects that the class is studying that students work on when they have extra time during class. They provide meaningful work for students when they finish an assignment or project, when they first enter the class, or when they are stuck on part of a task and are waiting for assistance. In addition, they free up the classroom teacher to work with groups or individuals while giving others something meaningful to work on (Tomlinson, 2001).

The following are examples of anchor activities pertaining to reading instruction. Students can (*Anchor Activities*, 2000):

➤ Write a letter to the author of a book they enjoyed.

➤ Read a biography about the life of someone they are interested in, and write a one-page summary of key events to present to the class.

➤ Create an original dialog between two characters from a book they are reading.

➤ Compare and contrast two books written by the same author.

➤ Decide upon a new ending for a book that they have recently finished reading, and write out the details of their idea.

➤ Create one or more illustrations that would go well with a book they are reading.

➤ Work on Accelerated Reader programs or other reading activities requiring the use of a computer.

Teachers can use anchor activities in a variety of ways. For example, the teacher may work with one group of students while another group works on an anchor activity. After a given amount of time, the teacher switches groups so that all students have time working with the teacher, as well as working on the anchor activity. The teacher also has the choice of allowing all students to work on the same anchor activity while differentiating instruction when working with the small groups of students. Or the teacher can allow the students to work on different anchor activities as well as differentiating instruction when working with the groups.

As an additional option for gifted readers who have pre-tested out of the basal text and are ready to move forward to something more challenging, the teacher can assign a trade book to read. He or she creates a schedule in which the gifted readers work with the teacher for one-third or one-half of the class time on activities related to the trade book, while the rest of the class continues working in the basal text on basic skills. The teacher then allows the gifted readers time to work on an anchor activity of their choosing while he or she works with the other students.

As you skim through the pages of Chapters 4 and 5, you will see a wealth of activities that can be used as anchor activities. (Additional anchor activities can be found in Tomlinson, 2001.) You may want to tab these activities so that you can easily locate them throughout the school year. One teacher uses red page tabs to indicate anchor activities appropriate for advanced learners and green tabs to indicate those appropriate for students needing reinforcement. The tabs help her when doing long-term planning.

Learning Centers

Learning centers are collections of activities or materials that promote or reinforce particular skills. They come in all shapes and sizes. Teachers often use centers to foster independence and goal setting. They can help facilitate differentiated instruction by addressing student interests and abilities, as well as provide opportunities to enrich curriculum. Teachers have the freedom to choose the types of centers and the materials in them that will best meet the needs of their students.

Most teachers, at some point in their careers, have used learning centers in their classrooms. The key to success with centers is to ensure that all students have opportunities to work in the centers and that the centers themselves are differentiated—by using a variety of materials, some with greater complexity, and by selecting materials that reflect different students' interests and ability levels. Carol Tomlinson (2001) writes, "Interest centers can provide enrichment for students who demonstrate mastery with required work and can be a vehicle for providing students with meaningful study when required assignments are completed" (p. 100). Students appreciate the opportunity to participate in centers because it eliminates their becoming bored when they have finished their regular classroom work.

Interest centers allow students to (Tomlinson, 2001, p. 100):

➤ Have some choice in how they learn

➤ Study with greater breadth and depth, satisfying their curiosity as they explore "hows" and "whys"

➤ Study topics not found in the regular curriculum

➤ Make connections between fields of study and life

Using Centers with Gifted Readers

Teachers who wish to meet the needs of their gifted readers will certainly want to use centers in their classrooms. The list below will help you get started:

➤ Administer interest inventories to help determine interests among students.

➤ Gather materials that will tap into those recorded interests.

➤ Determine if your centers will focus on writing, math, science, art, reading, or a combination of some or all subjects.

➤ Gather materials and activities that will meet your needs and your purpose.

➤ Be prepared to adjust centers by manipulating the materials to match student readiness and ability.

➤ Always explain the rules for using centers to students.

➤ Determine answers to the following questions:
  ○ Will students be permitted to work in centers after their regular work is completed?

○ Will students be able to pre-test out of certain lessons and then proceed to center work?

○ Will students work in pairs, teams, or independently?

○ How will students be held accountable for their work?

○ Will students' work completed in centers be graded, and if so, how?

○ If students have questions during their "center time," what should they do?

Examples of Centers

Centers can help differentiate reading instruction for gifted readers. Suppose that the whole class is reading *Grandfather's Journey* by Allen Say, which is a story about a man from Japan who travels to America, then returns to Japan to start a family, and ultimately goes back with his wife and daughter to live in America. As students complete their reading assignments for the day, they proceed to one of five centers. Gifted readers will go to the centers marked 1 and 2 and will have the following assignments:

➤ Center 1: First, locate Japan on a map. Next, using resources in the center, answer the questions on the white index cards about Japanese culture.

➤ Center 2: Using the orange and yellow cards, play vocabulary match-up in English and Japanese. Write a story, substituting some of the English words with Japanese words.

In Chapters 4 and 5 of this book, you will notice that there are many activities that can be used as centers for each book title. You might want to mark those activities that meet specific needs of your students or that correspond with stories found in your basal texts. Using centers with gifted readers is an excellent way to promote advanced learning while also using the basal reading text. In addition, this helps to ensure that no learning gaps occur while you practice differentiated instruction, because all students still participate in the basal reading program but have opportunities to complete work in centers designed to meet their individual needs.

Tiered Activities

Carol Tomlinson (2003) describes tiered activities or assignments as the "meat and potatoes" of differentiated instruction. Tiering activities simply means separating them into levels of increasing difficulty, with students working on those assignments that are appropriate for their ability level. Teachers can use this instructional strategy to help students explore ideas that build on their prior knowledge—however extensive or limited that may be—which prompts continued growth, no matter where on the continuum each student begins.

Most experts agree that three tiers are usually best when implementing tiered assignments. Teachers must first assess their students by using a variety of ongoing assessment tools to determine appropriate ability levels for the tasks being assigned. They must then place each student in a tier level, making sure to identify the goals and objectives that the group in each tier will be responsible for completing. As a guide for teachers, Tomlinson (2001) advises: "When task difficulty and skill level are slightly above student level, real learning occurs" (p. 35).

In this way, tiered assignments give all students opportunities to begin learning where they are and yet also allow them all to work with appropriately challenging tasks. Teachers avoid assigning work to students that is too hard, causing anxiety, or work that is too easy, causing boredom. In addition, instruction and assessment are combined (Tomlinson, 2003).

Virtually any schoolwork in just about any subject can be tiered. Assignments that are to be completed in class, homework, and activities that follow whole-group instruction can all be separated into tiers so that students can do work that challenges them at their level. A simple example follows.

Group 1:   Read _____.

Answer questions.

Write a summary to be included in our class newsletter.

Group 2:   Read _____.

Create a new ending to the story. Write and then read your new ending to the class.

Group 3:   Read _____.

Write a one-page paper telling why you think the character _____. In your opinion, did he/she do the right thing? Explain your point of view.

Questioning

We already know that gifted readers learn at a faster pace than their peers and should be exposed to information that continually adds to their knowledge base. Expanding that knowledge base involves teaching gifted readers to question, as well as to respond to higher-level questions.

Questioning is a valuable part of the teaching and learning process because it enables the participants—teachers and students—to establish what students already know, to use and extend this knowledge, and then to develop new ideas (Painter, 1996). Using higher-level questioning with gifted readers increases these students' awareness, fosters logical thinking, and promotes decision making through evaluation methods. In short, questioning is a critical strategy that helps gifted readers understand literature.

Jo Painter (1996) cites the following benefits for using questioning with gifted students. Questioning:

➤ Provides a structure to examine ideas and information

➤ Is integral to developing reflective and metacognitive awareness—in other words, students are thinking about their thinking

➤ Requires students and teachers to reflect on their understandings and can lead to changes and improvements in learning, thinking, and teaching

Questioning remains one of the most effective instructional tools in classrooms. It requires no extra materials or supplies, is easy to implement, and provides teachers with credible data about their students that can be used over an extended period of time. Most educators understand the benefits of questioning. Their only uncertainty is: "How do we implement this strategy so that it is effective in our classrooms?"

How to Use Questioning with Gifted Readers

To begin, teachers should examine the wealth of questions found in the basal reading texts; they can be a guide to help teachers ensure that gifted readers are learning and maintaining the skills needed to take standardized tests and to meet the benchmarks established by most school districts.

The kinds of questions asked are important. Many questions posed in classrooms today require only that students give a yes, no, or short response. While these types of questions are sometimes appropriate, they are not effective when used on a continuous basis with gifted readers, who are capable of responding to more complex questions and giving more thoughtful answers. With this in mind, classroom teachers should try to use more open-ended, complex questions—those which require gifted readers to analyze and evaluate characters' actions and decisions, thematic elements, and other more subtle or intricate elements of a story.

Types of Questions for Gifted Readers

Teachers can meet different students' needs by varying the difficulty of the questions asked. A useful resource in this task is Bloom's Taxonomy of Thinking (Bloom, 1956), an organized structure of thinking that progresses in levels of complexity. Questions at the lower levels—knowledge and comprehension—help teachers determine what children already know or have learned. Questions at the middle levels—application and analysis—encourage students to think more creatively and critically, applying the knowledge to other situations and comparing and contrasting different things. Questions at the highest levels—synthesis and evaluation—ask the students to delve even deeper into their thinking, such as making judgments and coming up with new solutions to problems. Teachers can use all levels of questions with all learners. However, it is important to ensure that gifted readers have plenty of opportunities to reach the higher levels of thinking and questioning.

Learning the different levels is important for teachers as they create questions for their students. The following chart will help you understand how to incorporate effective questioning into your students' learning. It is easy to see how knowledge and comprehension questions (often simple recall of facts and information) are easier than the higher levels of questioning that involve analysis, synthesis, and evaluation. Gifted students enjoy these higher levels of thinking and questioning versus the simple knowledge or recall questions.

> *Note: All students should be given opportunities to reach higher levels of learning through the use of appropriately developed questions. However, this must be accomplished only when students are ready to complete such tasks.*

Bloom's Taxonomy of Thinking	
Higher-Level Questions	**Evaluation:** form and defend opinions and make judgments based on criteria
	Synthesis: modify, generate, extend, and put parts of information together to form a new whole
Mid-Level Questions	**Analysis:** compare, contrast, categorize, examine, and take apart information
	Application: organize, explain, discuss, and solve problems by applying new information gained
Lower-Level Questions	**Comprehension:** demonstrate understanding by organizing and comparing
	Knowledge: recall facts, events, and terms

Adapted from Bloom (1956)

When asking gifted readers questions that relate to a book that they have read in class, remember to move them to higher-level questions when they can easily answer knowledge and comprehension questions. On the other hand, if there are readers who demonstrate a lack of understanding regarding story elements, be sure to ask them questions about the plot, characters, setting, or other important elements related to comprehension. This is the beauty of using questioning as an instructional strategy—teachers have the flexibility to move up and down the hierarchy of levels in order to meet individual students' needs.

One note about using the higher levels of questioning with gifted readers: Gifted students often prefer to learn globally, starting with the big questions or the larger themes—the big picture. In fact, many teachers find that these students prefer to work backwards—that is, they start with judgment and evaluation of the big picture and then work back to the knowledge, comprehension, analysis, and application types of thinking that they need to support their opinions, evaluations, and judgments.

The sample questions on the next page demonstrate how educators can begin to incorporate Bloom's Taxonomy of Thinking into the development of their discussion questions.

Sample Questions for Bloom's Taxonomy

Level 1: Knowledge	Where and when does the story take place? Describe the main character in the story. List and describe the other characters. Which character _____?
Level 2: Comprehension	How would you explain the meaning of _____? What can you say about _____ (character) from what you've read so far in the story? How would you summarize Chapter 3? How did _____ happen?
Level 3: Application	Are you like any of the characters in the story? Explain. How could you tell a friend about _____? What examples can you find that _____ (character) is changing? Role-play the discussion between _____ and _____ when they talk about _____. Is there anything about the setting of the story that reminds you of a place you know? Explain.
Level 4: Analysis	What is the main theme in this story? Compare it to another story you've read. How is _____ (character) different at the beginning of the story as compared to the end? What motive did _____ (character) have? What evidence in the story tells us _____?
Level 5: Synthesis	What changes would you make to help solve _____? How would you best describe the relationship between _____ and _____? How would you improve the story? Invent or create a plot similar to the one in this book.
Level 6: Evaluation	Were there any parts in the story that you did not like? If so, explain. Would it be better if the character had _____? Tell why. Would you recommend this book to a friend? Why or why not? Why do you believe the author chose to write this story?

Ways to Use Questioning with Gifted Readers

The following simple, effective questioning strategies will help gifted readers build their understanding and apply that new understanding to their everyday lives.

➤ Several gifted readers read the same teacher-assigned trade book independently. The teacher then provides time for these students to participate in a literature discussion group, during which they discuss teacher-developed questions. It is helpful if the teacher participates in the discussion group, at least the first few times.

➤ After reading a trade book independently, advanced readers receive a folder containing questions that are open-ended and require higher-level thinking. Students answer the questions and then give their folder back to the teacher for assessment. Alternatively, one or more students can have a conference with the teacher to share and discuss their responses to the questions.

➤ The teacher reads an appropriately selected trade book aloud to *all* students in the class, reading a chapter a day. After each chapter, students take time for reflection by answering teacher questions, either orally or in writing. Students who need extra practice in areas such as comprehension and application receive assignment sheets containing these types of questions to answer. Gifted readers receive assignment sheets that contain questions based on analysis, synthesis, and evaluation.

➤ After reading a selected trade book, gifted readers can play "quiz games" in a *Jeopardy* or other game show format using questions that they have developed, as well as ones the teacher develops. (A parent volunteer can be a big help in monitoring the quiz game in this situation.)

➤ Teachers can encourage higher-level learning in gifted readers through the use of journals, in which the teacher poses questions and the students respond in their journals.

Socratic Seminars

This instructional strategy dates back to ancient times and is, in essence, another way of using questioning. It is especially effective to use with gifted students. Students read one or more assigned books or excerpts of books and then gather in a group to discuss a question posed by the teacher. This question is open-ended and typically addresses some moral or ethical dilemma proposed by the works that the students have read. It is one that requires them to debate the issues based not just on what they can cite from the texts, but also on what they know from their own experiences in order to support their positions. They question each other and sometimes even change their minds. This is the essence of the Socratic method: "Through doubt and systematic questioning of another person, one gets to ultimate truth" (Tredway, n.d.).

During the Socratic seminar, the teacher's role is to keep the discussion going "along fruitful lines—by moderating, guiding, correcting, leading…" (North American Division Office of Education, 2010). However, the teacher should not engage in the conversation beyond this level—this discussion belongs to the students. To do this, the teacher should (North American Division Office of Education, 2010):

➤ Keep students from having side conversations.

➤ Ask students to cite support from the text [if] the conversation begins to wander.

➤ Invite students to participate.

➤ Keep conversations from becoming debate or debasement of others.

➤ Ask students to question their assumptions.

➤ Manipulate the amount of participation. For example, if only a few students are speaking, the teacher might say, "Everyone who has spoken so far, look at the clock, and don't jump in for five minutes." Or if one gender is dominating the conversation, ask for the other to speak for the next five minutes.

➤ [If] the conversation is truly dying out prematurely…ask the students…to summarize or comment on what they have heard. Ask them to re-introduce the points they thought were especially good or prematurely dropped. This strategy can often reignite the conversation.

Socratic seminars require gifted students to use their higher-level thinking skills as they evaluate options, make decisions, think critically about concepts, and analyze their moral principles. Perhaps most importantly, the students are engaged in these seminars on an emotional level, which makes the lessons both more enjoyable and more memorable (Willis, 2009).

An added benefit to this type of learning is that the students become skilled at relating to one another with respect. Some of the primary elements of Socratic seminars are that participants are strongly encouraged to listen carefully to others without interrupting, to paraphrase another student's ideas before responding to them, and to look each other in the eyes and use each other's names while holding this dialog. "This simple act of socialization reinforces appropriate behaviors and promotes team building" (StudyGuide.org, 2009).

Creative and Critical Thinking Cards (CCT Cards)

Creative and Critical Thinking Cards, or CCT cards, are cards that contain questions that correspond to the different levels of Bloom's Taxonomy of Thinking. Teachers create questions formulated to meet various student needs in the classroom, targeting specific learning objectives by providing questions based on different levels of thinking. These questions require the students to explore, evaluate, make judgments, and analyze decisions. The use of CCT cards will enhance any curriculum and help differentiate instruction.

If teachers use the cards in learning centers, they may choose to color-code specific questions based on the ability levels of the students. This helps to differentiate instruction based on ability needs. Differentiation also occurs when students make choices based on their interests as to which cards to complete.

Examples of CCT Cards

Creative and Critical Thinking Card # 4

1. What is your favorite holiday to celebrate? Tell why.

2. What do you think is the most important holiday? Explain your answer.

3. You have been given the opportunity to create or invent a new holiday. Think of a name for it. When and how is it celebrated? What is celebrated? Are there any symbols or traditions associated with your new holiday? Is any history related to your new holiday?

Creative and Critical Thinking Card # 36

1. The moon goes through many phases. Use a sheet of paper to show the different phases of the moon. You may use books or the Internet to find information.

2. You have been asked to ride on the next space shuttle traveling to the moon. You may take only five items with you. Make a list of the five items and tell why you chose each one.

3. Do you believe that the government should continue to supply money to aid future trips to the moon? Whether you answer yes or no, tell why. If your answer is no, tell how you feel that money could be better spent.

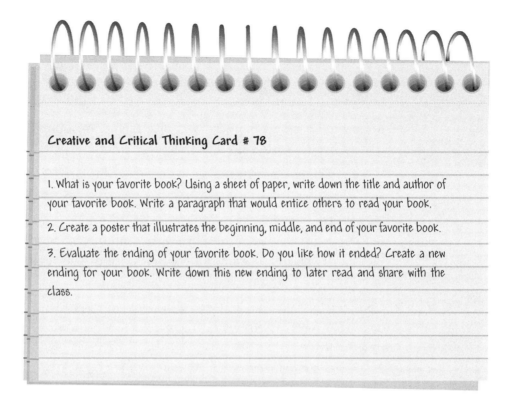

Creative and Critical Thinking Card # 78

1. What is your favorite book? Using a sheet of paper, write down the title and author of your favorite book. Write a paragraph that would entice others to read your book.

2. Create a poster that illustrates the beginning, middle, and end of your favorite book.

3. Evaluate the ending of your favorite book. Do you like how it ended? Create a new ending for your book. Write down this new ending to later read and share with the class.

After reading a book about Abraham Lincoln, a teacher could create several CCT Cards like the one below to reinforce facts and information about this important president.

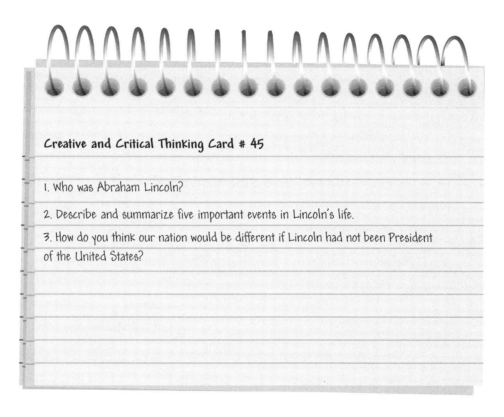

Creative and Critical Thinking Card # 45

1. Who was Abraham Lincoln?

2. Describe and summarize five important events in Lincoln's life.

3. How do you think our nation would be different if Lincoln had not been President of the United States?

How to Make CCT Cards

CCT cards can help teachers accomplish many learning objectives. If you would like to make your own cards to meet the needs of your students, here are some suggestions:

➤ Use index cards or small pieces of paper that can be easily recognized and that can fit into an appropriate container.

➤ Review the basal reading text, and pick themes or topics that are found in the reading book. Create CCT cards that focus on those particular themes.

➤ Write questions that spark students' interests while at the same time meeting students' learning needs.

➤ Become familiar with Bloom's Taxonomy of Thinking (see the section on questioning in this chapter). Use active verbs from the different levels of thinking on the chart to create questions for your index cards—for example, *compare, determine, critique, judge,* and *evaluate.*

➤ Consider goals that you have established for your students, as well as goals the students may have established for themselves. Ask yourself these questions: *Do my students need more in-depth study in particular areas? What types of materials do my gifted readers enjoy reading? What skills need to be reinforced? Do my students know how to make judgments based on something they've read? Can they evaluate these judgments and make recommendations based on their beliefs?* Create questions that relate to your thoughts.

➤ Make sure that your cards allow for questions that require higher-level thinking. Simple questions that require simple answers based on comprehension are fine, but gifted readers need more. If you are using CCT cards with a mixed-ability classroom, you may want to color-code the questions by ability level, assigning specific questions to specific students. All students, however, should be permitted to answer higher-level questions when they are ready.

Examples of Questions for CCT Cards

Here are some generic questions to use with CCT cards that can be adapted to any situation or topic:

➤ What do you think is the most important _____? (*analysis, evaluation*)

➤ If you were given the opportunity to _____, what would you do? (*application, evaluation*)

➤ Do you believe that the government should _____? Why or why not? (*analysis*)

➤ In your opinion, what is the best _____? (*analysis, synthesis, evaluation*)

➤ Locate three famous _____ and tell about them. (*comprehension*)

➤ What rules should people follow when _____? (*application*)

➤ List all of the things you can do in a _____? (*comprehension, application*)

➤ Create a new way to _____? (*application, synthesis*)

➤ Expand on the idea that _____. (*application, synthesis*)

➤ Judge the actions of _____. What is your opinion? (*evaluation*)

➤ What advice would you give _____? (*analysis, synthesis*)

➤ Pretend that you have been given a _____. What would you do with it? (*application*)

Ways to Use CCT Cards

Creative and Critical Thinking cards can be used in various ways:

Anchor Activities:	CCT cards can be used as anchor activities. As students complete learning contracts, independent projects, or regular classroom work, they may choose specific cards to complete for credit. These cards become their anchor activity for that week during reading.
Learning Centers:	CCT cards make wonderful learning centers. Complete a set of CCT cards, and place them in a box with paper and pencils. Allow students to go to the box when they complete their regular classroom work.
Journals:	Use CCT cards as springboards to journal entries. Ask students to go to the box containing the CCT cards and choose a question or topic to answer or respond to in their journals. Provide time for students to share their answers.

Flexible Grouping

Many of the differentiation strategies listed in this chapter require grouping students. Flexible grouping strategies allow teachers to meet individual needs by informally grouping and re-grouping students in a variety of ways (Valentino, 2000). Groups can be determined by ability, size, or interest. For example, a teacher may choose to establish a few different reading groups based on students' ability levels. Students reading at grade level are assigned a grade-level book, students who are struggling are given a more basic text to read, and advanced readers are assigned a book that is more challenging and contains more difficult vocabulary. Teachers who use flexible grouping can assign different projects that relate to the different books, thus creating an even more differentiated learning environment.

The use of flexible grouping allows teachers to move students forward in their learning while maintaining the freedom to rotate them through various groups in order to meet their needs. This makes grouping an excellent way to meet the needs of gifted readers, as well as to differentiate instruction. Here are three basic organizational patterns for grouping students.

Teacher-Led Groups

This grouping strategy maintains the classroom dynamic of teacher as facilitator, but by breaking the class into smaller groups of students, the teacher can become more intimately involved in each student's ability to progress. In most circumstances, the teacher works closely with one group while the other students work on projects that have been assigned to their group. The teacher then rotates to the next group, and so on until all groups have been given specific attention by the teacher. A class of 25 students may have four or five groups.

Student-Led Groups

These groups can take many forms, but they all share a common feature—students control the group dynamics. Below are three examples of student-led groups:

Collaborative groups: This is similar to cooperative learning in that students learn together by sharing ideas.

Circle sharing: This student-led group takes place in large circles. The leader, usually a student, gives the group an open-ended question, statement, or problem. Students take turns responding with ideas for possible solutions.

Four corners: In this grouping approach, the teacher poses a question or problem that contains four points or solving strategies. Students choose which part they want to help solve and then move to the designated corner of the room for their part of the problem. In this way, students practice working together as a team to solve a problem.

Performance-Based Grouping

"Sometimes groups of students with similar needs might benefit from additional support in the completion of a task" (Valentino, 2000). This can be accomplished with performance-based grouping, which can include both teacher-led and student-led approaches.

Unlike traditional ability groups, performance-based groups form for a short time and are used to respond to a particular need. For example, a teacher might find that, after reading a particular book, several students in the class are having difficulty completing questions or a vocabulary task related to the reading. The teacher can group these students together so that they can either work collaboratively to complete the given assignment or so that they can work on activities that will help them build the knowledge or skills necessary to complete the original assignment.

Conversely, the teacher may find that some of the students finish their work rapidly and accurately and have an abundance of time left over after regular assignments are completed. The teacher can pull these students into another group and give them extension or enrichment activities relating to the book.

Both of these groups of students—the students who are having trouble and the students who finish their work with time to spare—are then returned to the whole-group setting of the classroom for the next lesson. If similar issues arise during that lesson, the students may be re-grouped for further differentiated instruction. Note that performance-based grouping is a form of flexible grouping, meaning that a student who is grouped because of high performance in one area may be grouped with struggling students in another area. In this way, instruction becomes highly differentiated and individualized for each student in every subject.

Literature Discussion Groups

Another strategy to help differentiate reading instruction is to use literature discussion groups. Halsted (2009) suggests this strategy for groups of students who have read the same book and are generally around the same age and ability level. In group discussions, gifted readers can evaluate characters and debate issues found in the story. This strategy works well with all learners, regardless of ability levels, as long as the teacher ensures that the students who participate understand the rules for taking part in the discussion.

To set up a literature discussion group:

➤ The teacher should assess the students in the class and then group them according to ability. (Alternatively, a school librarian could organize these groups, drawing students of similar age from more than one classroom.)

➤ The teacher then chooses a book for each group to read.

➤ Each student reads the assigned book independently and at scheduled times.

➤ Discussions may take place two or three times a week, depending upon the length of the books. Teachers have the flexibility to decide how much time should be spent each week, as well as the duration of each of the discussions.

➤ The teacher establishes the general focus areas for the literature discussion groups. Examples are:
  ○ Character analysis
  ○ Setting, plot, and sequencing
  ○ Dialogue between characters
  ○ Identifying conflicts and solutions, then evaluating those solutions
  ○ Questions focusing on open-ended responses

➤ The teacher may choose to have students first discuss the questions and then write out their reflections on paper. In this way, the teacher can ensure that everyone participates.

➤ The teacher monitors each group's discussions, looking for:
  ○ Participation among group members
  ○ The group's ability to stay on task
  ○ Each student's ability to ask appropriate questions
  ○ The group's ability to debate in a positive manner
  ○ Each student's ability to demonstrate knowledge about the book read

Literature discussion groups promote reading and discussion skills in all students. The key to the success of these groups, however, is the grouping strategy that the teacher uses. To facilitate optimal learning, gifted readers should be grouped together so that they can feel safe in verbalizing and sharing their insights, and so that they can be challenged by each other. Through the use of appropriate grouping, teachers can provide gifted students with advanced coursework, as well as a peer group of other gifted students (Rogers, 2006).

Teacher Conferences

Teacher conferences between the teacher and each student can help to differentiate instruction because they keep the lines of communication open. The teacher can establish a timeframe in which gifted readers will read a particular book (one that the teacher has already read), whether they do so independently or in a group setting. The teacher then sets up individual conferences to promote dialogue between herself and the student—in effect, a literature discussion group of two. Alternatively, small-group meetings with gifted readers and the teacher can be just as effective, as long as the teacher ensures that each student participates in the discussions.

These conferences can be scheduled during times when other students are reading from the basal text, and they can be used to predict outcomes, analyze and evaluate decisions and actions of characters, and discuss important themes in the book. Teachers can also use questioning in these meetings with their gifted readers to facilitate discussions based on higher levels of learning. Examples of questions to use for teacher-student conferences are:

1. Why do you believe the author chose to name the main character _____?
2. Are there any parts of the story that you do not understand? If so, what parts?
3. What do you believe to be the main conflict in the story?
4. How might the author change or re-state the problem in the story?
5. So far, what is your opinion of the story? Why?
6. Is there anything in the story that relates to your own life? Explain.
7. Has the theme in this story changed any of your beliefs? Why?

Teacher conferences open the lines of communication and lead to advanced learning in the classroom. They also provide teachers with valuable data that can be used to assess students' levels of understanding.

Reading Buddies

To employ this strategy, the teacher pairs two gifted readers so that they can conduct their own discussions or team meetings. During scheduled times, reading buddies read their books together, share their thoughts, devise a list of questions that they want to consider further, make predictions, read passages together, research given topics, and discuss and analyze the meaning of certain quotes. The teacher acts as a facilitator or "coach" and encourages the students to respond to and reflect about the book they are reading in fun and creative ways.

This is an excellent way to promote relationship-building in gifted students, who sometimes have a hard time finding academic peers in their classes. It is very important, therefore, for the students to have reading buddies with whom they can establish a good rapport. Reading buddies can choose team names, team logos, team songs, team colors, and more. They can even be students at different grade levels. For example, if you have a student in third grade who is reading on a fifth- or sixth-grade level, you may be able to work something out with the fifth-grade teacher to find a reading buddy from the fifth-grade classroom. There are many different ways to use reading buddies with gifted readers. Give it a try!

Role Play

Teachers of gifted readers can review various reading skills by asking students to participate in a variety of role-playing situations. For example, students can identify the conflict in a story and then perform a short skit to teach the class about the conflict. It is always interesting to have the students predict how they feel the conflict will be solved and to include their prediction in the skit. Such role play promotes planning and organizational skills, while also allowing gifted readers time to express themselves in creative ways.

Read, Rotate, Record

This method gets the students up and moving—literally! It is one of my favorite activities. The teacher chooses two books that relate to a specific subject, such as art and art appreciation. One book is considered to be at grade level, while the other book is more advanced. Students who are reading at grade level read book A, and advanced readers read book B. If the teacher only has one copy of each book, the students read as a group, with one student reading aloud. If a teacher has multiple copies of these books, students read their books individually.

Before students read the books, the teacher places four sheets of large paper around the room. She shows the book covers and titles to the class. The students *read* the titles and talk about what they think the books might be about. The teacher then tells the students that they will *rotate* around the room and *record* things they may already know about the topic on the large sheets of paper. The students keep rotating and adding information until the sheets are full of facts and terms related to the subject at hand.

After the students have read their books, they again rotate around the room, recording information they learned on new, clean sheets of paper, each of which contains a different header. For example, one sheet might have at the top: "*Artists who worked during the 19th century,*" while another might say, "*Techniques used to create Impressionistic paintings*"; another might say, "*My opinion of Impressionism,*" and so on. In the end, the teacher pulls the students back into a whole-group setting to discuss the notes that are written on the sheets of paper. The teacher compares and contrasts the facts provided by the students, encouraging the students to identify opinions among the facts listed, noting which ones are supported by facts. This can serve as the springboard into a new lesson or unit related to the topic found in the books and in the curriculum.

Another approach to this activity is to use a variety of books from the library that relate to the same concept. The students work in groups, or they can work by themselves, reading selections from the books provided. The teacher might allow the students to focus on one book, or she might choose to have the students exchange the books after having them for just 5-10 minutes. This time limit encourages students to read for information, skimming the material for basic facts and interesting points, because they know they will be asked to show understanding as they rotate around the room.

Another suggestion is to organize the information on the sheets of paper into categories. For example, a yellow highlighter could identify information related to art media, and a green highlighter could indicate information related to artists. In this way, ideas that are interconnected among different subtopics can be discussed as aspects of the same main topic. Students like seeing the final product.

Still using our example of art, the four sheets of paper for *read, rotate, record* might look something like this:

Artistic elements that you recognize
- Brush strokes
- Color
- Lighting
- Perspective
- Shading

Names of artists
- Degas
- Cezanne
- Monet
- Morisot
- Van Gogh
- Seurat

Products in art
- Portraits
- Self-portraits
- Landscapes
- Still lifes
- Sculpture

Your opinion of art
- Art is fun
- Art tells a story
- Art requires skill
- It is calming
- It reminds us of things we know

Reading Box

For this activity, the teacher or a parent volunteer makes and decorates a reading box—perhaps a shoebox with a six-inch slot in the lid—that will be kept in the classroom. As gifted readers read certain books, they can ask questions or make comments on index cards and place those cards in the reading box. This idea is appropriate for all learners; however, gifted readers in general truly enjoy expressing themselves by writing their thoughts and ideas on the cards.

To help students better understand the books they are reading, teachers may also choose to write questions on the cards, which can be kept near the box. These questions can be differentiated by ability level, as well as interests. As students read their stories, they can select a card that corresponds to the book they have read, complete the questions, and then place the card in the box for the teacher or parent volunteer to review and respond to. Or the teacher can have classmates choose cards near the end of the class period and read the responses to the class.

Journals

Providing the time and resources needed to help gifted readers respond to literature can be challenging, but the use of journals can help ease this frustration. Teachers are encouraged to use journals with gifted students as often as possible during reading instruction to allow students to reflect on given stories, examine their thinking, make predictions, and express their thoughts and feelings in writing.

Journals come in many forms; they can be simple spiral notebooks purchased at local office supply stores, teacher- or student-created journals made from paper stapled together, or even something fancier. Similarly, there are many ways in which to use journals. Different kinds of journals help meet different educational needs. The following sections describe several types of journals.

Free-Write Journal

This kind of journal allows students to write in any manner they choose. A free-write journal is a place where students can feel free to write about any topic or event, or they can respond in it to questions provided by the teacher. Free-write journals are also fun when used with partners. Students can write to their journal buddy, and the buddy then responds. This is an easy way to get middle school students writing and thinking about their communication skills.

Critical Thinking Journal

Don't panic; it's not as bad as it sounds! This journal is simply a place where readers respond to the teacher's questions. The teacher develops questions pertaining to a particular book or topic of discussion using Bloom's Taxonomy of Thinking (described in the questioning section of this chapter). He or she then gives the questions to the students to answer within the pages of their journals, presenting gifted students with higher-level questions that challenge them. Critical thinking journals can be used with any subject.

Literature-Prompt Journal

Similar in style to critical thinking journals, literature-prompt journals are specific to reading instruction and are used in an ongoing basis while students are reading a book. Students are asked at given points in a novel to respond by writing in their journal. The prompts are tiered, from basic prompts to more advanced ones, and teachers assign them to students depending upon the students' ability levels, thereby differentiating reading instruction. An example follows.

Tier 1 Prompts

Describe where this story takes place.

Do you have a favorite character? Tell about your favorite character, and explain your choice.

What do you think is the most important part of this chapter? Why?

Make a list of the main events.

Make a chart showing _____.

Tier 2 Prompts

Compare yourself to the main character.

Identify a theme in this chapter.

Explain how the main character changed in this chapter.

Provide your own theory for why _____ decided to _____.

If the main character decided to _____, how would this change the story?

Tier 3 Prompts

What evidence can you find in the story to show that _____ was an honest person?

Generate a list of questions you would ask the author of this story.

What events in the story justify the character's decision to _____?

Change or modify the plot in order to make the story different. Write a plot outline showing the changes.

What judgment can you make about _____?

Synthesis Journal

In this type of journal, students analyze information to see how it relates to the "bigger picture." This information can be facts or even new perspectives learned from the books that they read. Asking students to examine information and ideas allows them to apply what they have learned to their own lives and determine how best to use this new information.

Sample synthesis journal

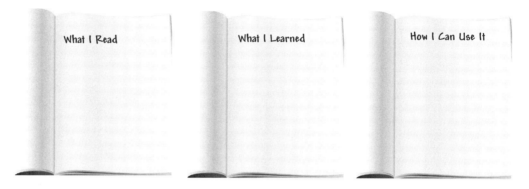

What I Read

What I Learned

How I Can Use It

Response/Reflective Journal

This type of journal is used to encourage students to record their thoughts and feelings about events in stories or characters' actions. It allows students to reflect upon and evaluate whether those actions were appropriate or inappropriate. For example, in the story *Archibald Frisby*, by Michael Chesworth, Archibald's mother sends him away to camp against his wishes. Students may read this story and then write in their journals whether they agree or disagree with his mother's decision, explaining their reasons. Response/reflective journals give gifted readers opportunities to use the higher-level thinking skills of analysis, synthesis, and evaluation.

Multiple-Entry Journal

This style of journal gives students opportunities to record and respond to text spontaneously as they read; they make entries whenever they choose as parts of a story pique their interest. As a result, students tend to focus on characters and their words or actions. Students then list these elements, along with their reactions to what they have written.

Sample multiple-entry journal

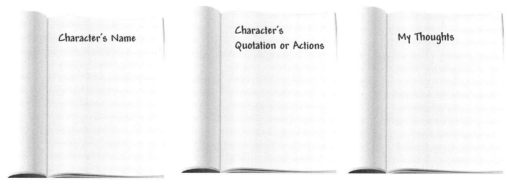

Character's Name

Character's Quotation or Actions

My Thoughts

Prediction Journal

This type of journal is particularly useful when students are reading an assigned book. The students can stop at different points in the book and make predictions in their journal about upcoming parts of the story. Predicting is a good reading comprehension strategy, which is useful when students take standardized reading comprehension tests.

Sample prediction journal

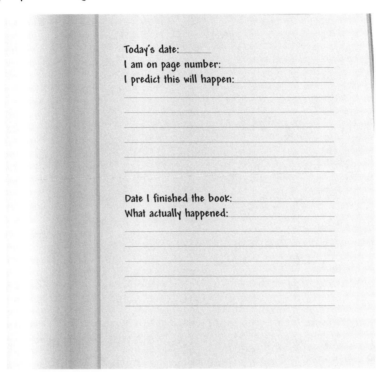

Quotation Journal

Some books are filled with quotations that are meaningful because they are profound, cryptic, or just plain funny. This kind of journal encourages students to reflect on quotations found within a story by asking them to spot them, analyze them, and decide how they might affect the rest of the story.

Sample quotation journal

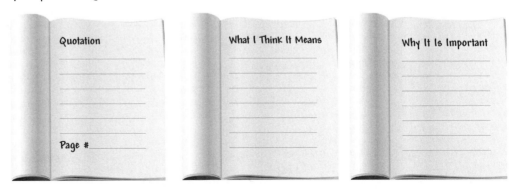

Illustration Journal

This is a great journal to use at any grade level, but it is particularly useful with gifted readers in the younger grades, since illustration journals allow students to read a book and then respond by drawing illustrations pertaining to the story. Older students can both write about events in the story and then illustrate them as well.

Comprehensive Journal

This style of journal is for teachers who like to keep everything neat and tidy and in one place. It contains individual sections which are tabbed for easy access. These sections are set up like chapters in a book and might include, but are not limited to, the following:

➤ Difficult Vocabulary
➤ Quotations
➤ Character Analysis
➤ Cause and Effect
➤ My Own Thoughts and Opinions
➤ Notes

How to Use Journals in Classrooms

➤ Decide which type of journal best fits the needs of your students and helps meet your educational goals for them.

➤ Model ways to use journals to ensure that students learn how to date every entry and write more than one or two sentences.

➤ Establish a regular time during reading instruction for students to write in their journals.

➤ Decide if journals will be graded, and make clear your guidelines and criteria for grading them. This is very important!

➤ As a teacher, keep a journal yourself to show students that you feel it is important.

➤ Try to integrate journals into other activities and subject areas. They can serve many purposes, including critical thinking and writing practice.

➤ Allow time for students to share their favorite journal entries with the class, if they feel comfortable doing so.

Graphic Organizers

Graphic organizers are among my favorite strategies to use with gifted readers. They help students become aware of their own metacognition—or in other words, to "think about thinking." Using these tools with gifted readers allows them to "chunk their learning" into categories, which helps to promote retention of material, as well as expansion of learning.

Martha Larkin (2001) says that graphic organizers can be used to:

➤ Help students locate and remember key facts and ideas
➤ Introduce and/or rearrange text information
➤ Strengthen written and spatial arrangement of information
➤ Summarize text, chapter, and units
➤ View information as a meaningful whole
➤ Help see inter-relationships among ideas
➤ Act as study guides
➤ Provide alternatives for test formats

For the purposes of this book, I have included some examples of the different types of graphic organizers, but there are many more available to help teachers meet the needs of their students. Teachers can search the Internet or ask colleagues to discover other types of graphic organizers.

Chain of Events

This type of graphic organizer helps students list the sequence of key events in a story. Teachers can create two separate sets of these kinds of organizers. The Level 1 organizer will work with all students. Students for whom this is too easy can work with the Level 2 organizer, which looks the same but requires students to use higher-level thinking. Modifying the graphic organizer in this way is an example of differentiation, in which the teacher gives advanced students more challenging work.

Sample Chain of Events (next page)

Directions: *Think about the book we just read in class. What happened in the beginning of the story? What happened in the middle? At the end? You certainly can't write down everything that happened in the book. Therefore, you must decide how to select and paraphrase the most important or key events so that a prospective reader will have a better understanding of the book after reading your comments. Make sure you include your favorite part for each section.*

Chain of Events

Level I

Beginning:

Favorite Part:

Provide "doodles" or simple drawings to show what takes place in these sections of the book.

Middle:

Favorite Part:

Provide "doodles" or simple drawings to show what takes place in these sections of the book.

End:

Favorite Part:

Provide "doodles" or simple drawings to show what takes place in these sections of the book.

Level II

Name of Character:

Actions in the Beginning:

Impact on Story:

In your opinion, was this a positive or negative impact? Explain.

Name of Character:

Actions in the Middle:

Impact on Story:

In your opinion, was this a positive or negative impact? Explain.

Name of Character:

Actionas at the End:

Impact on Story:

In your opinion, was this a positive or negative impact? Explain.

Storyboards

This kind of graphic organizer asks students to recall major events in a story and then illustrate them. In order to do this, students must evaluate the events of each chapter and decide what was significant. As students use their evaluative skills, they make decisions about actions portrayed by characters in the story. This information can then be transferred to a storyboard that requires the students to visually represent their assumptions made about these characters.

To help them get started, the teacher should encourage students to evaluate information found in the book. To do this, teachers may create short worksheets like the ones here.

Chapter 1

Name of character: _____

Traits displayed in Chapter 1:

Positive or negative character traits? Explain.

Chapter 2

Character traits displayed in Chapter 2:

Changes in character traits since beginning of book:

Impact these changes have on the story:

Chapter 3

Character traits displayed in Chapter 3:

Dynamic or static character?

Your predictions for how the character will appear in future chapters:

Storyboards are helpful tools for students who can read whatever is put in front of them but have difficulty illustrating major events. While some gifted students can read with ease, they are not always proficient when asked to visually represent what they read. Storyboards will help with this.

Sample Storyboard

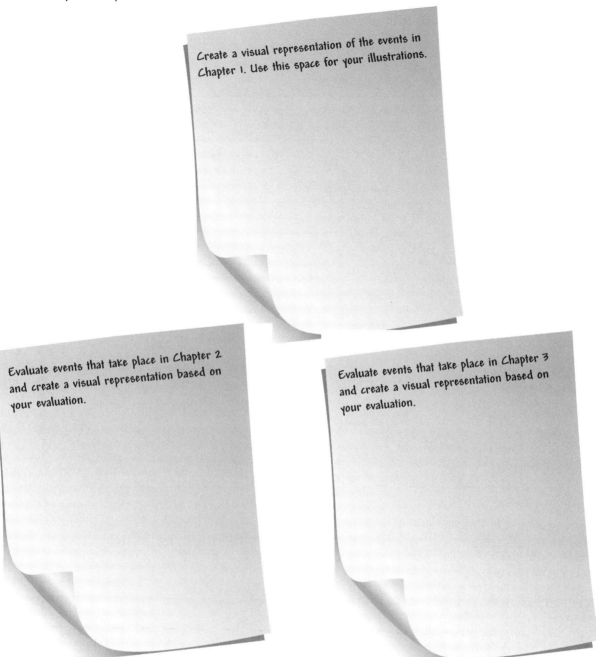

Problem-Solution

Understanding what happens in the text of a book that causes conflict in the story is an important skill for students to learn. This type of graphic organizer allows students to think through the problems in a book to their ultimate solutions. They can evaluate the problems and solutions after having read the book, or they can propose their own solutions before they read them in the text. This is a good way to get students to think about where a storyline may go. Gifted students in particular may find themselves excited to discover if their predictions are correct, and they will be developing their problem-solving skills in the process. A sample problem-solution organizer appears on the next page.

Problem-Solution Graphic Organizer

Name: _____ Date: _____

Title of Book: _____ Chapter: _____

| Identify a problem in the story: | → | What happens in the story to cause the problem? |

Which characters are involved in the problem?

Evaluate how the problem can be resolved.

| Identify another problem in the story: | → | What happens in the story to cause the problem? |

How does this problem differ from the problem stated above?

Which problem do you believe to be more critical to the story? Why?

Clustering/Semantic Maps

This style of graphic organizer gives students opportunities to brainstorm a variety of ideas about a story. This kind of "clustering" is particularly effective when students use it to gather ideas prior to working on writing activities. Some teachers call this "webbing" because it can look like a spider web of connected ideas. It can be used as a whole-class activity or assigned to be completed by individual students.

As an example, if the book that the students are going to read is about the Pony Express, the teacher might use this type of organizer to brainstorm facts and ideas about this early form of America's mail delivery system before reading the book. During and after reading, students can create another one of these organizers to document story elements.

Sample Clustering/Semantic Map

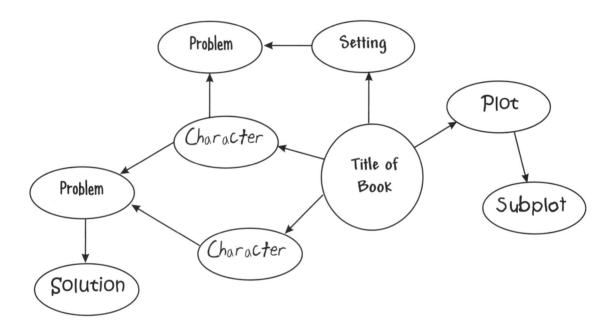

Venn Diagrams
This popular graphic organizer usually consists of two or more circles that overlap. Venn diagrams give students opportunities to analyze, compare, and contrast characters, settings, plots, etc. Venn diagrams are also helpful as a pre-writing tool to help organize thoughts, or they can be used after reading a book to compare character traits found in the story.

Sample Venn Diagram

Directions: *Choose two characters in the story and list traits for each one. Record how these characters are alike and how they are different.*

Character #1:_____ Character #2:_____

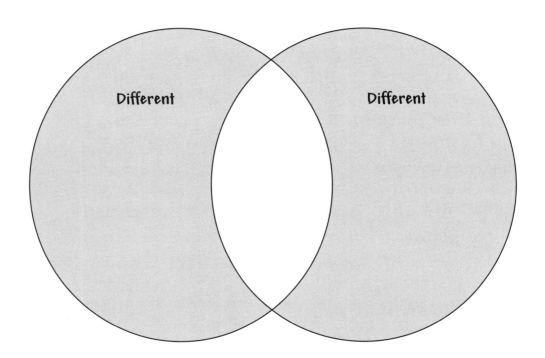

Ripple Effect

Some events create a ripple effect, much like what happens to a body of water when a stone is thrown into it. This style of graphic organizer is best used when trying to represent how an event in a story can affect the rest of the story by changing a major character's actions and behaviors, or even thoughts and emotions. Teachers should ask the students to think about the book that they are reading in class. What in the story do they think created a ripple effect?

When using this type of organizer, teachers can also ask students to provide examples of events in society that have had a ripple effect. This might relate to civics, the economy, or even current events in their community.

Sample Ripple Effect

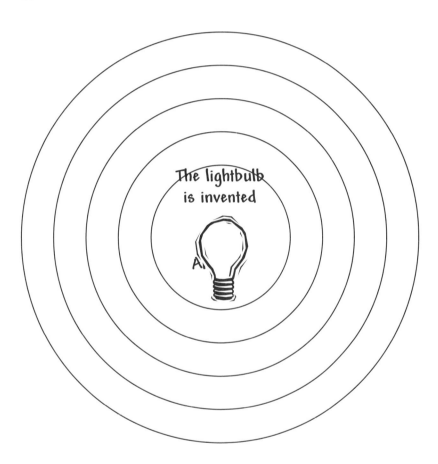

Discussion: *What effect did the invention of the lightbulb have on America, families, education, the economy...?*

Here is another example:

Ask students to name a recent environmental or political news event that has had a ripple effect. What about the economy? Write on the board "Wall Street collapse." Ask students to brainstorm the effect of that event (stocks lose value; interest rates rise; credit freezes; banks foreclose on homes; people lose confidence; people get angry; some are homeless; people stop shopping; people start saving; stores start having deep discount sales; some stores close), and for each thing listed, then write the effect of *that*. Before you know it, the board is filled!

Guidelines for Helping Gifted Readers Complete Graphic Organizers

➤ Teach students to use graphic organizers as a way of "chunking" information and organizing their thinking. Explain why these tools are so important—for example, students may later want to use these tools in high school classes for note taking or studying for exams.

➤ Provide examples of graphic organizers on chart paper and hang them in the classroom.

➤ Model the use of graphic organizers on a regular basis. For example, you might read the book *If You Give a Mouse a Cookie*, by Laura Joffe Numeroff, to the class. After reading it, create a "chain of events" graphic organizer to help students sequence the events of the story, completing the chart on the board while asking the students for help. After finishing the graphic organizer, ask the students to write a new story titled *If You Give a Dog a Bone*. Have them complete their graphic organizers before writing their stories.

➤ Allow gifted readers time to create and design their own graphic organizers and present their creations to their peers.

Some educators prefer not to use graphic organizers because they believe them to be too similar to "worksheet instruction." However, when used properly, graphic organizers give students new ways to see, think, organize their thoughts, and extend their thinking. The effectiveness of graphic organizers truly depends on the educator's ability to implement them.

🖉 Key Points

1. A differentiated classroom contains different elements so that the needs of all learners are met.

2. Differentiating instruction is important because it provides gifted students with challenging assignments and activities, which they often do not receive from the basal text.

3. There are many ways teachers can differentiate reading instruction for gifted readers.

4. Teachers should begin by examining their current reading programs to help establish a clear focus before implementing differentiated reading strategies.

5. When differentiating instruction, keep in mind that reading assessment needs to be ongoing so that teachers can assign lessons and activities based on students' current ability levels.

Chapter 4
Using Trade Books with Gifted Readers

> *Without complexity, gifted minds are less likely to remain actively engaged.*
>
> – Bertie Kingore

Complex Thinking and Responses

Teachers often do a good job of encouraging gifted readers to select literary works that are better suited to their reading level and other learning needs. However, it is what teachers ask these students to do before, during, and after their reading that requires attention. Gifted students need to have opportunities to delve deeply into literature and literary themes, as well as respond to thought-provoking questions.

Certainly, teachers have difficulty finding time to plan lessons that meet the needs of every student in their classes. Consequently, they often resort to asking gifted readers to respond to basic, knowledge-level questions about their reading that require only simple recall. This can be a dangerous instructional strategy with gifted students, as they can easily become frustrated with work that is not challenging. Despite time constraints, teachers, if they are to promote positive change, must find ways to facilitate, design, create, implement, and assess reading assignments that increase both depth and complexity of learning for their advanced readers. This book will provide many suggestions for these seemingly daunting tasks.

Putting Theory into Practice

The titles described in this chapter and the next are ones recommended by professionals in the field of gifted education. They are well-written books that address themes and issues that adolescent gifted students frequently struggle with, such as differentness, relationships with others, identity, and moral judgment. These books will engage gifted readers in literature that offers complex plots and characters, some of whom encounter great challenges or misfortune in their lives. Reading about how these characters have managed to overcome obstacles can help gifted readers who may face similar problems.

Chapters 1, 2, and 3 of this book contain information for classroom teachers as they learn to identify gifted readers, select appropriate literature for them, and incorporate instructional strategies that will enable these students to reach their full potential. Chapter 4 and Chapter 5 put theory into practice by recommending specific titles with a variety of activities that require gifted readers to stretch their thinking, encouraging them to look beyond simple, correct answers while forcing them to think differently about their learning.

Every teacher approaches instruction differently, and when teachers examine educational resources, they often look at them through very different lenses. For this reason, please think of Chapters 4 and 5 as "well-prepared buffets" that include something for everyone. Teachers should look for titles that match their current curriculum while also helping to meet the social and emotional needs of their students. Once teachers choose a title, they should review the activities and discussion questions, altering them as necessary to match their students' ability levels. These activities are meant to be flexible; teachers should adapt them to suit their own needs. In addition, most of the activities can be adapted for use with any of the other three books discussed in these chapters, as well as with many other trade books that are suitable for young adults.

The major benefit of these next two chapters is that, with the exception of minor alterations, the work of planning for advanced readers is done for teachers, which should make time constraints less of an issue. As they try the different activities and strategies, teachers will gradually become more comfortable with the concept and process of differentiation until it becomes second nature to them.

The Book Folio

A book folio is a collection of activities that are used not only to assess comprehension and increase understanding of a given story, but also to help teachers differentiate instruction in regular classrooms. Teachers can create a book folio for each of the four books that are discussed in Chapters 4 and 5. Keep in mind that these activities are meant to be modified to better meet the needs of individual students, and teachers are not expected to assign all activities to all students.

To make a book folio:

1. Photocopy the pages of activities for one or more of the books that are discussed in Chapters 4 and 5.

2. Put these pages in a binder or folder to use throughout the study of that particular book.

3. Instruct students to work on selected activities during specific time periods. Teachers may choose to have advanced readers complete the activities while other students work on regular classroom assignments. These activities may also be used in learning contracts, activity menus, or learning centers.

A Note about Vocabulary

An essential element of reading is understanding vocabulary words, being able to recognize them in books, and becoming familiar enough with them to use them in everyday speech. Within the pages of Chapters 4 and 5, you will find a list of vocabulary words for each of the four books discussed. Learning these words will help students understand their reading, and becoming comfortable with them will allow students to read literature of increasing difficulty.

When teaching students new vocabulary words, it is important to keep it fun and interesting. Teachers should avoid overwhelming students with a huge list of words prior to reading the book; this can sometimes turn off readers before they even get involved in the story. Lists of vocabulary words can be more of a help to middle school readers if these students have an opportunity to do something with the words to help remember them. Students who have a chance to manipulate information retain it better than those who just passively read it (Willis, 2009).

The vocabulary activities in these two chapters will not only help develop students' vocabulary, they will also generate interest in the stories and give students a sense of the literary themes interwoven in the texts.

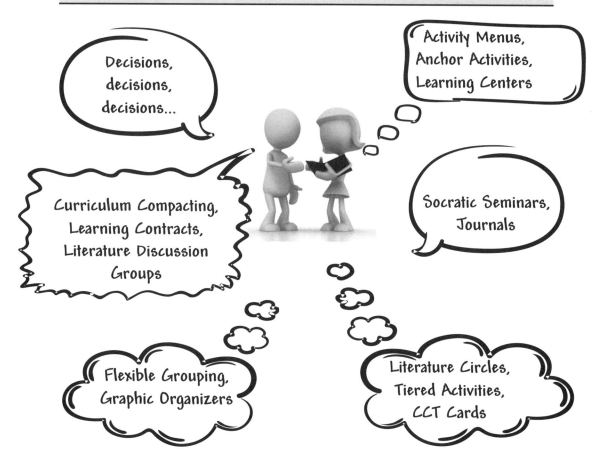

Extending Literature:
Understanding perspective, making inferences, dissecting conflicts, constructing evaluative meaning, and synthesizing key concepts

Decisions, decisions, decisions...

Activity Menus, Anchor Activities, Learning Centers

Curriculum Compacting, Learning Contracts, Literature Discussion Groups

Socratic Seminars, Journals

Flexible Grouping, Graphic Organizers

Literature Circles, Tiered Activities, CCT Cards

A Quick Reference of Titles and Activities Found in Chapters 4 and 5

Use this chart to help select appropriate books to use with gifted readers. Consider individual needs as you choose titles and activities.

Titles and Authors	Themes	Elements Included in Book	Activities
The Midwife's Apprentice, by Karen Cushman	Facing hardships, identity issues, developing friendships, finding self-worth and self-esteem	Set in medieval times; Old English dialect	Denotation and Connotation; Pre-Reading Learning Extensions; Pre-Reading Discussion Topics; Questions and Prompts Using Bloom's Taxonomy; Socratic Seminar; Discerning Fact from Opinion; Making Inferences; Analyzing Decisions
No Pretty Pictures: A Child of War, by Anita Lobel	Overcoming hardships, family separation, loss, resilience, wanting to fit in, discovering new talents	Historical aspects of the Holocaust; cultural elements, including words from other languages	Important Terms to Know Before Reading; KWL Charts and Pre-Reading Discussion Questions; Using Vocabulary; Reading Log; Making Predictions Based on Evidence; Human Needs Analysis; The "Snippet" Book Report; Whole-Group Discussion Prompts; Evaluating Quotes; Literature Extensions
Walk Two Moons, by Sharon Creech	Accepting difficult truths, empathy, family relationships, dealing with loss	Double plot—story within a story; American Indian cultural aspects	Developing Vocabulary; Literary Elements; Literature Circles; Discussion Questions and Prompts; Extension Projects; Literature Circle Forms
The Schernoff Discoveries, by Gary Paulsen	Friendship, courage, social rejection, trying to fit in, drive to understand	Irony and exaggeration for humorous effect	Expanding Vocabulary; Elements of Language; Discussion Questions and Prompts; Analyzing Quotes; Using Bloom's Taxonomy; In-Depth Discussion

The Midwife's Apprentice
by Karen Cushman

Summary

Set in medieval England, *The Midwife's Apprentice* is about a homeless young girl called Brat. She is discovered by the village midwife, who provides her with shelter and food in exchange for work. As Brat matures and gains confidence, several events unfold that help her become a strong young woman who knows what she wants out of her life.

A Newbery Medal award-winner, this book offers an in-depth view of life in the Middle Ages. The author's use of Old English dialect will challenge gifted readers, and they will enjoy the complexities of the book's plot and characters.

This book facilitates discussions about:

- Overcoming hardships
- Facing identity issues
- Using one's ability
- Drive to understand
- Developing relationships with others
- Learning self-worth and gaining self-esteem

The Midwife's Apprentice
by Karen Cushman

Vocabulary Words

The following vocabulary words are found in the book *The Midwife's Apprentice*.

stench	ranting	tumult
dung	meandered	privies
sties	quivered	lumpish
scrawny	solemnity	exertions
reeked	replenish	teemed
wimple	dire	mucking
moiling	daft	compendium
taunting	sheaves	sorrel
bedeviled	incautious	mayhap
reedy	paternosters	desolate
feverfew	deceit	abide
curdled	magpie	bleating
ragwort	bade	befouled
bryony	writhing	berating
haggling	mewling	prosperous
midwifery	betook	barren
dawdle	revelers	sullen
bellowed	befallen	devoured
nitwit	treachery	hasten
laden	thievery	surfeit
boneset	crooned	morsel

The Midwife's Apprentice
by Karen Cushman

Activity: Denotation and Connotation

Denotation is the dictionary meaning of a word, whereas the *connotation* of a word is the idea or feeling that is sometimes associated with it. Words can have positive or negative connotations. For example, a word with a positive connotation gives readers a good feeling. Words with negative connotations give readers bad or unpleasant feelings. Words can also have neutral connotations, which means that they trigger neither good nor bad feelings.

Examples: **Neutral**: overweight   **Positive**: portly, plump   **Negative**: fat, obese

Neutral: ask   **Positive**: request   **Negative**: demand

Directions: *The words found in* The Midwife's Apprentice *are rich and challenging. This activity will help you better understand many of the unusual terms you will find in the story. Choose 10 words from the vocabulary list you were given of words from the book. Record the words you chose in the chart below, and then write similar words that you feel have positive and negative connotations, like the examples above.*

Neutral Vocabulary from the Story	Positive Connotations	Negative Connotations

The Midwife's Apprentice
by Karen Cushman

Activity: Pre-Reading Learning Extensions

The author of *The Midwife's Apprentice* provides a note at the end of the story that explains the history of midwifery. Prior to reading the book, review Cushman's informative note with your students to provide important background information about the profession of women helping women who are going through childbirth. Students will better understand the story if they know that "Medieval midwifery was a combination of common sense, herbal knowledge, and superstition" (p. 119). Today we have many professionals who are trained in assisting women with childbirth.

Pre-Reading Discussion: Ask students if they believe in superstitions or know of anyone who does. A superstition is a belief arising from ignorance or fear that is passed from person to person through tradition. A discussion about superstitions, traditions, and midwifery will prepare students for reading and for the activities.

Tiered Assignments: For the assignments in this activity, students must be separated into three groups—one for each of the three activities. These groups can be based on interests or abilities, or the teacher can place the students in mixed-ability cooperative groups.

Activity 1. Brainstorming: Post a large sheet of paper on the bulletin board or wall, and ask the group of students completing this activity to create a graphic organizer in any style they choose (see Chapter 3) to expand upon their ideas for the word "superstition." They can record their own superstitions, their opinions about superstitions, and their analyses for whether or not superstitions can help or hurt people as they grow in life. They must then present their information to the class.

Activity 2. Midwifery in Different Countries: Students in this group will do Internet and library research to learn how to pronounce and write the word "midwifery" in different languages and to see how it is practiced in different countries. This group will then decide how to present their findings to the class. They must teach the others how to write and pronounce the word "midwifery" in different languages, as well as the word's exact translation to English. For example, the author tells us in the Author's Note at the back of the book that in France, *sage femme* means wise woman; in Denmark, *jordemoder* means earth mother; in Yiddish, *vartsfroy* means waiting woman; and in Hawaii, *pale keiki* means protector of the child. This group will also show where the different countries are located on a map.

Activity 3. Facing Hardships: The main character in this story faces frustrating situations that test her strength. This group will be instructed to determine what qualities are needed to achieve a goal despite tremendous hardships. After creating this list of qualities, they must evaluate which quality on the list is the most desirable to maintain when achieving goals, and they will be required to explain why they chose this quality as opposed to the others on their list. Finally, they must answer the following question: *Do you believe that people become stronger or weaker as a result of facing many hardships in their life?* They should consider health, living conditions, money, and so on, and then present their findings to the class.

The Midwife's Apprentice
by Karen Cushman

Activity: Pre-Reading Discussion Topics

Discussing Elements of Fiction

A discussion that reviews the elements of fiction will help generate student interest in the story. Fiction is a form of prose writing that tells a story using imaginary events. In fiction, we find invented characters (people, animals, creatures, etc.). These characters typically experience a sequence of events that make up the plot of the story. The plot usually begins when a conflict arises. The character must face the conflict within a particular timeframe and in specific locations, which are considered the setting. As the story progresses, the author might weave a theme throughout the storyline. This theme might serve to tell something about life or human nature, such as overcoming challenges or making self-discoveries that promote growth.

Making Predictions

Before reading this book, allow students to examine the front cover illustration. Then ask:

- ❍ Based on hints from the artwork on the cover, what do you believe this story is about? Why?

- ❍ What does the book cover tell you about the main character, the setting, a possible conflict, and the theme?

- ❍ Does this cover illustration remind you of any other stories you have read?

A brief discussion about making predictions based on illustrations and images will motivate students to read the book with some preconceived notions about the book's contents.

Analyzing Quotes from Text

Author Karen Cushman provides a powerful visual image in a quote at the beginning of the book on page 2:

> *Tonight she settled for the warm rotting of a dung heap, where she dreamed of nothing, for she hoped for nothing and expected nothing. It was as cold and dark inside her as out in the frosty night.*

Questions for discussion:

- ❍ What does the above quote tell you about the girl? Explain your answer.

- ❍ Why do you believe the author chose to give readers this information so early in the story? How does this impact your opinion about the story before reading the rest of it?

- ❍ From this quote, what will you remember as you read more about this young girl?

The Midwife's Apprentice
by Karen Cushman

Activity: Questions and Prompts Using Bloom's Taxonomy

This activity contains questions for each chapter of the book, as well as thought-provoking quotes for several of the chapters. These questions and quotes can be used as starting points for class discussions or journal entries, activities to help students connect with the story, prompts when using literature circles or Socratic seminars, or even as test questions. You will notice that each one is followed by the thinking levels it requires under Bloom's Taxonomy of Thinking. This will help you select higher-level questions for your advanced students. You will want to examine this list carefully before giving the book to students to read so that you can select the questions you want to use and then decide upon the best times to introduce them. Please don't give students the entire list of questions at once and ask them to respond as they read—the students do not need to answer every question, and giving them too many will take the fun out of their reading.

Chapter 1: The Dung Heap

1. Chapter 1 reveals many things about Brat's history, her relationships, her personality, and her self-esteem. Use the information you gained from this chapter to tell what you know about Brat. How does this information enable you to make judgments about her? (*knowledge, comprehension, analysis, synthesis*)

2. Explain how Brat becomes Beetle. How and why does her name change? If you had to choose a single adjective to describe Beetle, which one would you use? Do you believe her to be in a better situation at the end of this chapter than at the beginning? Predict what you think may happen next. (*knowledge, comprehension, application, analysis, synthesis*)

Chapter 2: The Cat

3. The mean boys take the cat that Beetle has befriended, put it in a bag with an eel, and throw it in a pond. Beetle hides behind a tree, afraid to help because she knows that the boys will taunt and tease her if they see her. After the boys leave, she takes action. Describe what Beetle does after the boys leave. What do you think was the author's purpose for including this scene in the book? Does the cat symbolize anything at this point in the story? Defend your answer. (*knowledge, comprehension, analysis, evaluation*)

4. Beetle and the cat have a lot in common. Compare and contrast them by listing characteristics they each possess. How do these characteristics make them similar or different in actions and mannerisms? (*knowledge, comprehension, analysis, synthesis*)

Chapter 3: The Midwife

5. Chapter 3 reveals information about the midwife. For example, we learn that her name is Jane. We also learn about some of her character traits. Jane seems to be excited that she has found someone to help her deliver babies who is considered stupid by others. Why does Jane prefer someone like Beetle as opposed to someone else from the village? Explain your answer using details from the story. (*knowledge, comprehension, analysis, synthesis, evaluation*)

6. When Jane is called to help women from the village who are in labor, she does not allow Beetle to stay in the cottage during the actual delivery of the baby. Is this a wise decision? Why is Jane so secretive about her midwifery skills with Beetle? Why doesn't she want Beetle to learn from her? Wouldn't it be a help to her if Beetle knew more? Evaluate this decision by Jane to keep Beetle from learning more about midwifery. (*analysis, synthesis, evaluation*)

7. The villagers are angry with the midwife's greed, but they don't show Jane their anger. Instead, they take their anger out on Beetle. What causes them to do this? Why can't they show their anger to Jane? (*comprehension, application*)

8. Now that Beetle is working for Jane, what do you believe she needs to learn about herself that will help her later in life? Why do you believe this? (*analysis, synthesis*)

9. Beetle's only friend is the cat. Does Beetle need human friends as well? If so, why? What does she need to learn so that she can make friends? (*analysis, synthesis, evaluation*)

10. Jane has various jars and jugs containing bizarre items and concoctions on her shelves. List the contents of some of the jugs, and then make an assumption about the purpose of these contents. (*knowledge, application, analysis*)

11. Beetle performs many tasks for Jane at this point in the story. List some of the tasks. Then, choose one of Beetle's chores, and compare it with a chore that you are responsible for at your home. (*knowledge, application, analysis*)

12. Describe four things that are different between life in medieval times and now. (*knowledge, comprehension, analysis*)

13. As the chapter ends, Beetle realizes that she has learned more than she thought. She begins secretly trying to learn more. Predict how this might affect her as the story continues. (*comprehension, analysis, synthesis*)

Chapter 4: The Miller's Wife

14. In this chapter, Beetle discovers a secret involving the midwife and the village baker. What is the secret? If you were in Beetle's position, would you have tried to find out why the midwife was acting so strangely? Why or why not? Is it wrong to spy on others to discover secrets that they don't want anyone to know about? (*knowledge, application, analysis, synthesis, evaluation*)

15. After she discovers the midwife's secret, Beetle returns home, talking to the cat the entire way. Why does she do this? What is the author's purpose for including this in the story? (*comprehension, analysis*)

16. The village miller summons for help as his wife lies in misery. The midwife is nowhere to be seen, and Beetle finds herself suddenly in charge. She is afraid, however, and curls up in a corner to hide. Luckily, the midwife suddenly appears and delivers the baby. Beetle returns home only to be punished. Tell what you believe to be a major weakness for Beetle at this point in the story. What advice would you give her if she came to you and described the events of the day? (*application, analysis, evaluation*)

Chapter 5: The Merchant

17. As Jane prepares to attend the Saint Swithin's Day Fair, she experiences an unfortunate accident. Describe this accident and what occurred as a result of it, and predict how this will affect Beetle in the rest of the story. (*knowledge, analysis, synthesis*)

18. Jane's misfortune brings joy to Beetle, as she is permitted to attend the Fair. At the Fair, a merchant gives her a wooden comb. Explain why this act of kindness surprises Beetle. (*analysis, synthesis, evaluation*)

19. "The wink and the comment about her curls, though Beetle didn't know it, were also gifts from the generous merchant, and they nestled into Beetle's heart and stayed there" (p. 30). The merchant's act of kindness seems to be a turning point in Beetle's life. Explain the meaning of the phrase, "they nestled into Beetle's heart." What does this mean? What effect does this event have on Beetle? (*analysis, synthesis*)

20. In this chapter, Beetle chooses to give herself a new name. What is this name, and why is this act significant? What does it say about Beetle? What has caused her to make this change? (*knowledge, comprehension, analysis, synthesis*)

Chapter 6: The Naming

21. Chapters 5 and 6 contain content that illustrates some transformations taking place in Beetle's life. Identify some of these changes, and tell why you believe them to be important as Beetle begins to mature. (*comprehension, application, analysis, evaluation*)

22. Authors use dialect to depict time periods, cultures, and locations. Locate passages in Chapters 5 and 6 in which the author uses dialect to indicate life in medieval England. Document some quotes, along with page numbers, so that you can discuss your findings with the class. Also, explain what you learn about medieval England as you dissect quotes from these chapters. (*application, analysis*)

Chapter 7: The Devil

23. Mysterious events occur in the village, causing fear among the people. "Suddenly the whole village saw witches and devils everywhere, and fear lived in every cottage" (p. 41). Explain why the village people feel such fear. Predict what you believe to be causing such a ruckus in the village. (*analysis, synthesis*)

24. Alyce is the only person in the village who is not frightened at night. Why isn't she afraid like the rest of the villagers? Is there more than one reason for her to be unafraid? (*application, analysis, synthesis*)

25. The villagers believe that the strange footprints leading to the church door are the Devil's. Why do you think they came to that conclusion? Interpret this thinking by applying your knowledge of medieval England. (*application, analysis, synthesis*)

26. Evaluate the title of this chapter: "The Devil." If you were given the opportunity rename this chapter, what would you choose and why? (*analysis, synthesis*)

27. Analyze this quote: "And so it was that all (except the fortunate midwife) who had taunted or tormented Alyce were punished for their secret sins. After this, the Devil was never seen in the village again, and no one but Alyce knew why" (p. 46). Who was punished? What were the sins? In the end, who was the person making the footprints, and what do you think this tells us about that person? (*knowledge, comprehension, analysis, synthesis*)

28. The midwife was the only person who was not punished. Do you think that the person punishing the villagers for their sins meant for Jane to be punished? Why or why not? (*analysis, synthesis, evaluation*)

Chapter 8: The Twins

29. After Alyce helps to deliver twin calves, Will Russet tells the villagers that she brought him good luck. Do you think that Alyce and Will will become friends? How do you think the other boys who used to tease her will treat her from this point forward? Predict how you think this event might help to change Alyce. (*application, analysis, synthesis*)

30. This chapter portrays Alyce as a growing girl who is slowly maturing. She acquires knowledge and skills that earn her respect from others. However, Alyce still doesn't see herself as a valuable individual, giving all of the gifts she receives from the villagers to the midwife. Why do you think Alyce does this? In your opinion, why doesn't Alyce realize how much she has learned? What does she still need to learn about herself? (*analysis, synthesis, evaluation*)

Chapter 9: The Bailiff's Wife's Baby

31. After Jane runs out on the bailiff's wife as she struggles to give birth, Alyce rises to the challenge by providing aid to the mother, using skills that she learned from watching both Jane and Will Russet. When the midwife returns for her pay, the bailiff says: "We have no need of you, Jane. Your helper has taken care of us with her two strong hands and her good common sense" (p. 60). Predict what will happen to Alyce for helping the bailiff's wife. Tell why you believe this. (*analysis, synthesis*)

Chapter 10: The Boy

32. Alyce decides to hide in the cottages and watch as Jane delivers babies. During this secretive time, Alyce learns about herbs—for instance, she learns that birthwort roots and flowers can strengthen contractions. List some of the other remedies for childbirth that Alyce learns about as she hides in the cottages. What is your opinion of the benefits of these remedies? (*knowledge, comprehension, evaluation*)

33. When Alyce goes to the barn to see the twin calves, she discovers something far more interesting. Tell what Alyce finds. (*knowledge*)

34. Evaluate Alyce's actions as she helps the small boy. Notice the character traits that she shows as she interacts with him. She defends him against the village boys, just as she had defended the cat in the previous chapter. What does this say about Alyce? Why is she now able to stand up to the boys when she never used to be able to? Why do you think she has changed this way? (*analysis, synthesis, evaluation*)

Chapter 11: The Leaving

35. Alyce runs away when the midwife delivers Emma's baby. Do you believe that this is a setback to the growth and progress that Alyce has made thus far in the book? Defend your answer with details from the story. Next, analyze the following quote: "…for she had never learned to give voice to what was inside her. She knew only to run away" (p. 70). What does this mean? (*knowledge, comprehension, analysis, synthesis, evaluation*)

36. Explain how Alyce handled her feelings of failure, and interpret why she had these feelings after making so much progress in life. (*comprehension, analysis*)

37. Alyce not only learns something about herself in this chapter, she learns something about Jane's skills as a midwife. Predict how this new awareness toward Jane might change their relationship. (*analysis, synthesis*)

Chapter 12: The Inn

38. Using the dialect found in this book, tell how Alyce feels about herself at the beginning of this chapter. If you could talk to her, what would you say to help? (*knowledge, comprehension, application*)

39. Was there ever a time when you felt like you failed at something? How did you react? What helped you overcome those feelings? (*application*)

40. Identify the location where Alyce ends up after leaving the village. Predict how this new setting will affect Alyce's life. (*knowledge, analysis, synthesis*)

41. The cat that Alyce befriended in the beginning of the book still plays a large role in her life. What important role does the cat play in this chapter? (*knowledge, comprehension, analysis, synthesis*)

42. Alyce stays at the inn for several months. Despite compliments about her work from the inn keepers, she still considers herself a failure. Find evidence in this chapter of Alyce's negative feelings about herself. Alyce utters a powerful statement at the end of

this chapter that demonstrates her perception that she belongs nowhere. Locate and copy this quote as part of your evidence. (*comprehension, analysis*)

43. Alyce meets a renowned scholar by the name of Magister Reese. Over the course of the winter, M. Reese teaches Purr, the cat, the letters of the alphabet. By overhearing his instructions to Purr, Alyce learns how to write. Why do you suppose M. Reese teaches the cat? What is he trying to accomplish? Next, when M. Reese finally speaks to Alyce instead of Purr, he asks her a question. What is it? (*knowledge, comprehension, analysis, synthesis*)

Chapter 13: Visitors

44. Will Russett delivers wood to the inn and gives Alyce the village news. The author leaves the reader wondering if Alyce is beginning to like Will and vice versa. Is this information important at this point in the story? Why do you believe this way? (*analysis, synthesis*)

45. Alyce wants to make up an excuse to tell Will about why she left the village, but she ends up telling him the truth. Why do you suppose she does this? Would she have told the truth to anyone other than Will? Will then says to Alyce, "Just because you don't know everything don't mean you know nothing" (p. 85). Do you think Will's words will change the way Alyce thinks about herself? (*comprehension, analysis, synthesis, evaluation*)

46. The midwife makes a visit to the inn, and Alyce overhears her conversation with Magister Reese. Jane speaks about her former apprentice giving up and not trying again after she failed. Jane continues her conversation, almost as if she knows that Alyce is listening. Evaluate whether you think that Jane knew Alyce was there and secretly hoped she was listening to her conversation. (*analysis, synthesis, evaluation*)

47. Determine Jane's purpose for visiting the inn. Use details about Alyce's previous visit with Will Russett in your explanation. (*knowledge, comprehension, application*)

Chapter 14: The Manor

48. Alyce sees Girtle nursing her newborn calf. This makes her want to see Edward, the small boy she found in the barn. Why do you think seeing Girtle and her calf made Alyce want to see Edward? What evidence in the story makes you believe this way? (*knowledge, analysis, synthesis*)

49. Alyce envisions Edward as a poor wretch whom she rescues from misery and takes care of, to his great relief and gratitude. She thinks that she "…would scoop the boy up in her arms and they would go together back to the inn and Alyce would take care of Edward and this would make her heart content. All she needed was Edward and all would be well" (p. 90). Why do you think that Alyce has such a strong desire to rescue Edward and care for him? What would make her believe that all would be well for her if that happened? (*analysis, synthesis*)

50. Alyce has feelings in her throat as she passes villagers working in the fields. What sort of feelings are they? Find a phrase in the chapter to support your opinion. (*knowledge, comprehension*)

51. The author weaves the theme of change throughout the story so that readers understand the growth made by the characters. What evidence is there in this chapter that Alyce is maturing? (*knowledge, comprehension, synthesis, evaluation*)

Chapter 15: Edward

52. Alyce longs to see Edward. Describe what she finds when she enters the hen house looking for him. (*knowledge*)

53. Examine this quote: "So Alyce learned about the sometimes mighty distance between what one imagines and what is" (p. 97). What does this mean? How does this relate to Alyce's finding Edward? (*comprehension, analysis*)

54. Emotions play a critical part during the reunion between Alyce and Edward. What emotions do you think were the most prominent in Alyce? In Edward? (*comprehension, analysis, evaluation*)

55. Readers see Alyce cry during her visit with Edward. This is a turning point for Alyce. What was the author's purpose for including this event in the story? Later in the chapter, the author says that Alyce "felt that tickling in her throat and stinging in her eyes that meant she might cry again, now she knew how to do it" (p. 103). Why do you think Alyce had to learn how to cry? (*analysis, synthesis*)

56. Alyce helps the village men wash the sheep in the river. This job leads to a new self-discovery for her. Tell what Alyce learns about herself after helping the village men and their sheep. (*knowledge, comprehension*)

57. The further we read, the more we see glimpses of the changes going on within Alyce. What is changing about Alyce? How is she different now than she was when she first came to the inn? (*knowledge, comprehension, application, analysis, synthesis*)

Chapter 16: The Baby

58. A woman arrives at the inn about to give birth. Alyce watches in secret, pondering the idea of helping this woman. All of the good things and the bad things that people have told her about herself crowd into her head. Finally she says, "Keep still, all of you, and let me try" (p. 108). What does Alyce mean by this? Who is she really talking to? What makes her ultimately decide to help? (*comprehension, analysis, synthesis*)

59. After a great deal of work, Alyce finally helps the woman deliver a baby boy. The men who accompanied the woman call Alyce an angel and a saint, and Alyce celebrates her accomplishment with a loud laugh. Why was this event important for Alyce? Does this symbolize something in the story? (*comprehension, analysis, synthesis*)

Chapter 17: The Midwife's Apprentice

60. Alyce is tempted with many offers—the rich merchant wants her to care for his son, M. Reese wants her to join him in Oxford to care for his ailing sister, and the inn keeper's wife offers to pay her a small amount now and then if she stays. If you were Alyce, what would you do? Defend your answer using information from the story. (*knowledge, analysis, synthesis*)

61. This chapter includes a quote that brings logic to Alyce's decision. As she asks herself what she should do, she says, "'Of course.' She was not an inn girl or a nursery maid or a companion to old women. She was a midwife's apprentice with a newborn hope of being someday a midwife herself" (pp. 113-114). Explain Alyce's decision and how she reached it. What do you believe the author meant by "a newborn hope"? (*analysis, synthesis*)

62. When Alyce goes to see Jane and tell her that she has returned to be a midwife's apprentice, Jane refuses her. This is a crucial point in the story. What is Jane attempting to get from Alyce? Why do you think this was this so important to Jane? Defend your answer with evidence from the story. (*comprehension, analysis, synthesis*)

63. Alyce goes off and sits with the cat. Suddenly, she jumps to her feet and says, "Jane herself told me what she needed" (p. 116). Determine what Alyce means by this statement. What did Jane tell Alyce, and when did this happen? (*knowledge, comprehension, analysis*)

64. Alyce knocks again on Jane's door and tells her what she now realizes Jane wants to hear her say. Determine how Alyce knew what Jane wanted from her. Are there parts within the story that indicate Jane wanted this from Alyce as far back as when they first met? Back up your responses with evidence from the story. (*knowledge, comprehension, analysis, synthesis*)

65. Now that you have finished reading and discussing the story, write a letter to the author. In your letter, tell what you found interesting, what you learned from reading the book, what you liked and did not like, which characters you thought were the most interesting, and anything else you'd like the author to know. (*application, analysis, synthesis, evaluation*)

The Midwife's Apprentice
by Karen Cushman

Activity: Socratic Seminar

The questions below are ideal for use in Socratic seminars (see Chapter 3 for information about Socratic seminars). These questions not only ask students to demonstrate their understanding of the book, they also encourage students to ponder and debate moral and ethical issues found within the story. An added benefit is that students learn how to discuss potentially volatile topics with courtesy and respect.

1. As Brat becomes Beetle and Beetle becomes Alyce, we see her transforming into something far greater than she could ever have imagined. Part of this transformation is because of the strength and courage she displays. If Alyce did not possess these qualities, how might the story be different? Show how Alyce changed from the beginning of the story to the end. Is there a lesson to be learned that we can all apply to our own lives?

2. Where and how does Alyce find the courage to begin changing her life? Are there certain events that help her to grow and change? If so, name two or three events that you think contributed to her growing self-confidence. Would these types of events have the same effect on everyone? On you?

3. Who helped Alyce in the story? Why did they help her? Did Jane actually help Alyce, or were there instances in which she did more harm than good? Do you think Jane was really trying to help herself when she was helping Alyce? Does it matter what a person's motive is if their actions help another?

4. Alyce exposes secrets about some of the village members. Do you think it helped the others in the village to know about these secrets? Do you think that, in the long run, it was good for the village members who had secrets to have them exposed? In your opinion, does everyone have a secret?

5. What is your opinion of Alyce's role in the village scare over the Devil's footprints? Why did Alyce get involved in this deception? Was it right for her to be involved in these actions? Was it harmful to anyone? Was there potential for harm? Was the outcome positive? Why or why not? How do we determine what is ethical and "correct" behavior?

6. What actions and events in this book raise issues about medical ethics? As a midwife, would any of Jane's behaviors be unacceptable in today's society? If so, why? Did Jane do anything that was unethical? Explain. Did Alyce do anything that was unethical? If so, what? And when?

7. When Alyce goes to visit Edward at the manor, Edward describes the life he has led there. In his description, he talks about people who live very luxurious lives for that time period. Compare this description with how Alyce and Edward live. What do you think of this disparity? In the Middle Ages, the wealthy people had servants to do all of the work for them. Can you think of any other instances in history that were similar to this situation, either in the U.S. or in any other countries? What happened to change this? Do we have situations like that anywhere in the world now?

8. Think about all of the characters in this story. Identify one character as a leader, and tell why you believe this person would be capable of leading others.

The Midwife's Apprentice
by Karen Cushman

Activity: Discerning Fact from Opinion

Directions: *Discerning facts from opinions in a story is important. Complete the following chart by providing three details from the story that are facts and three details that are opinions. Please include page numbers for the quotes or details that support your facts and opinions.*

The author includes the following facts and opinions in the story:

Fact:	Quotes or details that support these findings: Page #:
Fact:	Quotes or details that support these findings: Page #:
Fact:	Quotes or details that support these findings: Page #:
Opinion:	Quotes or details that support these findings: Page #:
Opinion:	Quotes or details that support these findings: Page #:
Opinion:	Quotes or details that support these findings: Page #:

The Midwife's Apprentice
by Karen Cushman

Activity: Making Inferences

Directions: *For this activity, you will make inferences and draw conclusions about Alyce. You must explain what kind of person Alyce is in the story. Locate three quotes from the book that reveal important aspects of Alyce's personality. Copy each quote into the table below, as well as the page number where you found it in the book, and then write what you think the quote means. Remember that Alyce changes as the book progresses, so be sure to include quotes that demonstrate her transformation. Later, we will compare and contrast your information with that of other readers.*

Alyce Says:	My Analysis:
I. Quote: Page #:	Meaning of Quote:
2. Quote: Page #:	Meaning of Quote:
3. Quote: Page #:	Meaning of Quote:
Use this space to write a summary about your opinion of the type of person Alyce was in the book, and how she gradually changed.	

The Midwife's Apprentice
by Karen Cushman

Activity: Analyzing Decisions

Alyce is treated badly by several people in the story. She gets revenge by deceiving the people in the village and convincing them that something evil is happening. Consider this statement:

Deceit is an evil act unless it is used to expose the deceit of others.

To make wise decisions, it is important to look at both sides of an issue. Complete this graphic organizer by reflecting on your thoughts and feelings about the statement above.

It is *sometimes* okay to be deceitful to others.	It is *never* okay to be deceitful to others.
Reason	Reason

Why did Alyce do what she did with the Devil's footprints?

Do you agree or disagree with Alyce's actions when she revealed the sins of those who treated her badly? Tell why.

No Pretty Pictures: A Child of War
by Anita Lobel

Summary

Anita Lobel holds nothing back as she puts her life into words so that others may understand the pain she experienced as a child in a concentration camp. In this memoir, Lobel candidly describes the life she and her brother lived as they hid with their nanny in Nazi-occupied Poland until they were finally caught and forced to become prisoners in a series of concentration camps during the Holocaust. As a special bonus, the book includes Lobel's own archival photographs.

Lobel tells her story using well-crafted language that engages readers. Her words are descriptive and evocative, allowing readers to see the settings through Lobel's own eyes. Historical aspects of the Holocaust are discussed, inviting teachers to use this book as a tool to teach history as well. The story will help students comprehend the circumstances of this time period, and it encourages them to form their own judgments about actions taken by those involved in this horrific historical tragedy.

This book facilitates discussions about:

- Overcoming extreme hardships
- Family separation
- Abandonment and loss
- Understanding different cultures
- Identity issues
- Wanting to fit in
- Resilience
- Discovering talents

No Pretty Pictures: A Child of War
by Anita Lobel

Vocabulary Words

The following vocabulary words are found in the book *No Pretty Pictures: A Child of War*.

concentration camp	barter	cadence
deportation	crevice	ethereal
liquidation	shellac	veranda
unison	matron	coherent
glinting	Aryan	tome
bayonets	menacing	cordoned
mutter	cowered	pristinely
Hasid	regimented	gaunt
ravine	urchins	prim
sneered	fervently	surliness
barren	berating	ebbing
rickety	taunted	officiousness
steins	edifice	lilting
dreary	foreboding	jubilation
desolate	averted	docile
cravats	reverberate	gauche
Semitic	acrid	treacherous
gesticulating	barracks	swarthy
confiscated	abyss	contortions
sloshed	lulled	tentative
wimple	pungent	render
balustrade	luminous	stigma
segregated	hoist	profusely
incriminating	vermin	periphery
indignant	furtive	

No Pretty Pictures: A Child of War
by Anita Lobel

Vocabulary Words

There are many words from other languages in this book. These words are Polish, German, and Swedish. If you know someone who speaks any of these languages, ask them to help you pronounce them. Here are many of the translations offered in the book:

tatuś = papa

Niemcy = Germans

Juden = Jews

droszki = horse-drawn carriages

kilim = long rug

servus = hello

pani = madame

ciocia = aunt

kogutki = little roosters

verboten = forbidden

lalki = dolls

makownik = poppyseed cake

kielbasa = sausage

kinder = children

schnell = fast

milch = milk

brot = bread

bitte = please

konzentrationslager = concentration camp

likwidacja = liquidation

rechts = right

links = left

bruder = brother

Herr = Mr.

pan = mister

pensionat = boardinghouse

fröken = Miss

fru = Mrs.

realskola = high school

akvareller = watercolors

affärselev = business student

No Pretty Pictures: A Child of War
by Anita Lobel

Activity: Important Terms to Know Before Reading

Before students read *No Pretty Pictures*, there are some important terms that they will need to become familiar with to understand the story. Copy this page to give to each student, and ask them to cut out the word cards. Then group the students into pairs or triads, and have them take turns pronouncing the words and reading the definitions. They can then fold the word cards and quiz each other on them. Afterward, they can paste or tape the cards into their journals.

Auschwitz	Concentration and extermination camp in Poland	**ghetto**	A section of a city where all of the Jews from the surrounding areas were forced to live
deportation	The forced removal of the Jewish people from their homes by the Nazis	**Holocaust**	The destruction of some six million Jewish people by the Nazis and their followers in Europe in 1933-1945
Final Solution	The name for the plan that would destroy all of the Jews in Europe	**liquidation**	The elimination of the Jewish people by the Nazis by putting them to death
genocide	The deliberate destruction of a religious, racial, national, or cultural group	**Resistance**	An underground organization that helped the Jewish people against the Nazis

No Pretty Pictures: A Child of War
by Anita Lobel

Activity: KWL Charts and Pre-Reading Discussion Questions

When preparing to discuss emotional topics, such as the subject of this book, it is important to provide time for students to make personal connections to it. Ask students to complete a KWL chart (What I <u>K</u>now, What I <u>W</u>ant to Know, and What I <u>L</u>earned) about World War II, the Holocaust, and concentration camps so that they can make connections to their prior knowledge. There is a KWL chart that you can copy and distribute to the students on page 98.

In the first column of their KWL chart, students should record things they already know about the Holocaust. They will use the second column to record things that they want to know about it. After discussing this topic with the students, allow them to record things that they learned during the discussion in the last column. The teacher can also choose to have the students leave the last column blank until after reading the book.

A group discussion of the Holocaust can cover many issues. Several questions follow that will help teachers direct this discussion.

How many of you have heard of the Holocaust? What is the dictionary meaning of the word? What other meaning does it have in history? Where and when did it happen? What country or countries were involved? What country was the aggressor? Who was their leader? How did Hitler become so powerful so fast? What are some things you know or have heard about the Holocaust? (Some students may have seen movies like Schindler's List, The Boy in the Striped Pajamas, Valkyrie, *or* The Reader *or read books like* The Diary of Anne Frank.)

Why did the leaders of the German army think they were doing the right thing? Do you think the German people all agreed with these leaders? Were there some people who protested? How did some of the Jews manage to escape? Do you know the story of Anne Frank? Did she and her family escape?

How did the German army actually carry out its plan? Describe how the Nazis took Jewish people to the labor camps and the extermination camps. Did the Jewish people know what was in store for them when they were taken to the camps? Do you know the names of some of the "death camps"?

Can you imagine how you might feel if soldiers came and told your family that you had to go live in a fenced-in area and give up your home, your business, and all of your possessions? Are there countries today where people are being mistreated and forced to live in refugee camps, away from their homes and normal way of life? Name some of these countries.

What do you think it is in human nature that causes countries to fight against one another, and in the case of Germany, to fight against some of its own citizens? Do you think there will always be war? What do you think could be done to stop wars and violence? Is there anything positive that comes from war? Give some examples.

Have you ever met anyone who survived the Holocaust and one of the death camps in Europe during World War II? If so, describe this person. Most of the survivors who were in their teens at the time would be in their 80s or 90s now. They would have a number tattooed on their arm. Why did the Germans give them a number tattooed on their arm?

After the discussion, the teacher can introduce *No Pretty Pictures* by Anita Lobel to the students in this way:

The book we are about to read was written by a woman who was a child during World War II. It contains her memories of those years when her family had to figure out how to stay alive with terrible events happening all around them. She survives and, years later, writes this book so that others can understand what it was like to be a young girl during these frightening times.

No Pretty Pictures: A Child of War
by Anita Lobel

KWL Chart for No Pretty Pictures
World War II, The Holocaust, and Concentration Camps

What I Know	What I Want to Know	What I Learned

No Pretty Pictures: A Child of War
by Anita Lobel

Activity: Using Vocabulary

Directions: *Learning new vocabulary words is more than just looking up definitions for them; it also involves learning how to use the words in everyday language. Look at the list of vocabulary words that you were given for this book. Choose eight of the words that you don't already know, and look up their definitions in the dictionary. Then, write a sentence using each word correctly, according to its meaning. You will write eight different sentences.*

For more challenge, try writing sentences using two of the words from the list. For even greater challenge, try writing sentences with three of the vocabulary words. Remember, the sentences must make sense.

When everyone has completed this activity, we will take turns reading our words and their definitions, as well as the sentences that we wrote. It may be interesting to see if two or more students wrote different sentences using the same words. When everyone is finished, we'll post our sentences on the bulletin board for the class to see.

1. Word:_____

Definition:_____

Sentence:_____

2. Word:_____

Definition:_____

Sentence:_____

3. Word:_____

Definition:_____

Sentence:_____

4. Word:_____

Definition:_____

Sentence:_____

No Pretty Pictures: A Child of War
by Anita Lobel

5. Word:_____

Definition:_____

Sentence:_____

6. Word:_____

Definition:_____

Sentence:_____

7. Word:_____

Definition:_____

Sentence:_____

8. Word:_____

Definition:_____

Sentence:_____

For More Challenge (Optional):

Sentence using two words:_____

_____

Sentence using two words:_____

_____

For Even Greater Challenge (Optional):

Sentence using three words:_____

_____

Sentence using three words:_____

_____

No Pretty Pictures: A Child of War
by Anita Lobel

Activity: Reading Log

Directions: *As you read* No Pretty Pictures, *keep this reading log to help you connect with the text, as well as to strengthen your understanding of the author's purpose throughout the story. Please include quotes, phrases, conversations, and scenes from the book. Also include page numbers, because we will share this information during our literature discussion groups.*

Examples of Fear	Examples of Courage	Indications of Values and Belief Systems
Page #:	Page #:	Page #:
Page #:	Page #:	Page #:
Page #:	Page #:	Page #:
Page #:	Page #:	Page #:

No Pretty Pictures: A Child of War
by Anita Lobel

Activity: Making Predictions Based on Evidence

Directions: *This book has many twists and turns. Sometimes Anita and her family seem safe, and sometimes they are in great danger. There is suspense throughout the book, because the reader isn't sure what might happen next. Predicting what will happen next is something that the reader does almost unconsciously.*

For the first part of this activity, choose a part of the book that you found suspenseful, write what you thought was going to happen, and then write what actually happened. Next, answer the other questions about what you predicted might happen in the story.

In Chapter _____, when _____,

I thought _____

_____.

What actually happened was _____

_____.

Here's what I thought would happen to Anita and her brother:

_____

_____

Here's what I though would happen to their friends and family:

_____

_____

What actually happened was:

_____

_____

No Pretty Pictures: A Child of War
by Anita Lobel

Activity: Human Needs Analysis

This is a *silent* activity. On the board or a large sheet of chart paper, write the words "Human Needs." Without giving any further information, tell the students that they will have 10 minutes to think of the many possibilities related to this particular concept.

As students think of ideas, they come to the board and write them. They will also be able to write responses to each other's words or phrases. For example, a student may write, "Food and drink are the most important needs." Another student may come to the board and respond by writing, "You have a good point, but I feel that all human needs are equal; if one area is not met, then the others will wither away." Then the first student can defend his statement. In essence, the students hold a debate by writing on the board. This is a good way for students to express their viewpoints and to learn ways to appropriately respond to comments and opinions made by others without heated verbal arguing.

After 10 minutes have passed, the teacher takes control of the board. She leads a discussion, making connections between all of the comments that are similar and circling all of the comments that are different. In this discussion, ask students questions such as: *What happens if certain needs are not fulfilled? How would you react if a law was passed that took something away that fulfilled a human need of yours? (For example, what if all cell phones were banned in public places and you could only use your phone in your home?) Think about the consequences that such a law would have on our society.* Ask students to brainstorm ideas for a new law that would take something away and that would have a huge impact on our society.

At the end of the discussion, students can talk about whether they've had a change of opinion about the most important human needs or if they still feel the same as they did in the beginning. They can also comment about things they learned from the process. These group discussions will promote higher levels of thinking, as students are forced to connect their personal opinions to facts that they can defend.

Finally, have students complete the "Hierarchy of Human Needs Chart," which appears on the next page. Once they have completed their charts, you may want to share Maslow's Hierarchy of Needs (Maslow, 1998) with them for comparison and discussion.

Hierarchy of Human Needs Chart
for *No Pretty Pictures: A Child of War*

Directions: *You must rank the order in which you think human needs fit into this chart. When making your decisions, you can consider the information that we placed on the board for the "Human Needs" activity, as well as the discussion that followed. You may start at the top or bottom, but you must provide evidence to defend your decisions.*

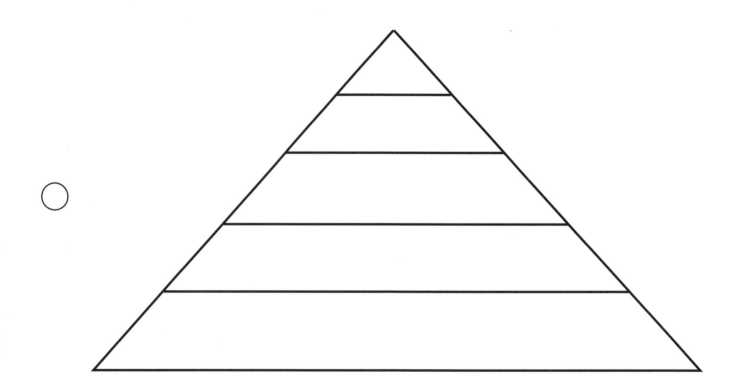

No Pretty Pictures: A Child of War
by Anita Lobel

Activity: The "Snippet" Book Report

This activity is a long-time favorite! It can be used with an entire class or with a group of six or more students. After the students have read the book, they should be prepared to give a detailed summary of it. The students will stand up and form a line around the room. The teacher begins the process by pointing to a student and saying, "Start!" The student starts telling about the beginning of the story, but before he finishes his summary, the teacher points to another student. That student picks up the story where the previous student stopped, adding more details. The teacher then stops that student and points to yet another, who picks up and relates her summary of the story from that point forward.

Middle school students love this activity because it gets them out of their seats, and it keeps them alert and thinking because they don't know when the teacher might point to them to continue the story. Gifted students particularly enjoy the process because it becomes more challenging the further it goes. Give it a try!

No Pretty Pictures: A Child of War
by Anita Lobel

Activity: Whole-Group Discussion Prompts

1. In this story, there is evidence that humankind is sometimes good and sometimes evil. Discuss episodes in the book that reveal that humankind is inherently good. Then discuss episodes that show examples of human behavior turning evil.

2. How do different cultures shape the definitions of good and evil? Think about the different cultures found in this story. Do you believe that this question can be answered fairly and without bias? Explain.

3. During the story, there are many decisions made that lead to specific consequences. For example, when the children's mother shows up in Niania's hometown, it causes suspicion, which then means that the nanny and children have to find another place to hide. What is the relationship between decisions and consequences? Think of two or more examples in which a person's decisions and actions can change his or her life. Then give two examples of how the decisions and actions among characters in this book reveal their personalities.

4. Discuss the part in the story when Niania takes the author and her brother to the home of the two peasants. The peasants give them food, but when they walk away from the house, the peasants throw a bucket of bodily waste on their heads. Why do they do this? Does it seem strange to you that they would do something nice and then something so nasty so quickly afterward? What is Lobel trying to tell readers with this scene? How is this scene important to the development of the author's struggles?

5. This book has many themes that bring up sadness for the reader. One of these is the idea of abandonment. The author and her brother are alone during some very scary situations. Her father had gone to Russia, and her mother sent her and her brother to live with their nanny separately from her. When the war was over, Niania moved away and never saw the two children again. How do these two young children cope with this abandonment? How does it affect them? Do you think that at any point in the author's life she ever overcame her feelings of abandonment? If so, when? And how?

6. Religion plays a large part in the author's story, primarily because it is her Jewish religion that causes her and her family, along with many others, to be sent to concentration camps. At several points in the story, the author wishes she weren't Jewish. She learns and embraces Catholicism from Niania and Protestantism from the Swedish. Does Lobel give us any clues as to what religion she most identifies with after she is reunited with her parents, or later, as she becomes an independent adult? Give evidence from the book for your answer.

7. As the war rages on, the author learns to trust nothing and no one—not even her family. There are several instance in the book in which her fear and paranoia take over, and she cannot and does not trust what she sees and hears. One example is the incident

when her aunt and cousin ask her to step away from the marching Jews in the dark of night. In the epilogue at the end of the book, Lobel tells us that she learned what happened as a result of her refusing to step away. What happened? How do you think Lobel feels knowing now what the consequences of her actions were? How would you feel? How do you think she has been able to deal with this terrible information over the course of her life?

8. At one of the concentration camps, a woman cuts off all of Lobel's hair. Even though all of the women have their heads shaved like this, the author is embarrassed and doesn't want anyone to see her naked head. What do you think the author was really embarrassed about? How does this compare to her brother being dressed as a girl for so long as a disguise to prevent suspicion from the Nazis? Do you think he was embarrassed? Give evidence from the story to support your answers.

9. During much of the book, the author and her brother experience feelings of fear and loneliness. There is one part of the book, however, where Lobel finally feels safe, secure, and even happy. Why was this, for her, a place of pretty pictures, even without her parents and her nanny there? Why didn't she want to leave to be with her parents again? Do you think her brother felt the same way? Find evidence in the book to support your answers.

10. Once Lobel finally gets to go to school in Sweden, she discovers that she greatly enjoys it and that she's very good at it. She is particularly good at learning languages and becomes fluent in not just Polish and Swedish, but also German and English. Later, she also discovers that she is an excellent artist. What do these discoveries tell her about herself? How do they help her? Do they hurt her in any way?

11. One of the skills of an author is to help the reader "see" the different scenes in the book and "feel" the emotions that the characters in that scene must have felt. What scenes or "pictures" from the story particularly stand out in your mind? Discuss some of the scenes that seemed like a frame from a movie because you could see them so well. Find one or more of these scenes in the book and examine it more closely. Describe the scene and the feelings or emotions you had while reading it. Do you think you would have felt the same way or acted the same way if you were in that same situation?

12. The author is an artist. She is very visual. It is remarkable that she can remember this part of her childhood in such vivid detail. Do you believe it was difficult for her to write this book? Why do you think she wrote it? Why did she title it *No Pretty Pictures*? Explain your answers.

No Pretty Pictures: A Child of War
by Anita Lobel

Activity: Evaluating Quotes

The following quotes from the book can be used for many different purposes—journal prompts, assessment questions, or prompts for literature discussion groups.

Poland

1. "Where is Tatuś?" I asked. "Why did Papa leave us?" "He had to. Jewish men are in more danger from the Nazis than women and children." (p. 7)

2. "Somewhere there must be a terrible place. A barren area with no light. With leafless trees and no blue in the sky. Where these words stopped being just words and became real things." (p. 9)

3. "…even leaving for a place I had never been, I felt a weight fall away from me when the wheels began to turn. The fears and dangers of the whole day dissolved and flowed into the newly greening branches of trees…." (p. 24)

4. "The whispers of the trapped grown-ups sounded like the noise of insects rubbing their legs together. Below us, above us, we felt the hushed lives of caged people." (p. 45)

5. "And then came the moment when we were once again shaken from our suspended time and were forced to think of hiding or running." (p. 45)

6. "…I felt surrounded by danger. I could feel it coming from the dusty clumps of bushes. From the path winding toward the distance. From the clouds in the sky." (p. 63)

7. "I wanted to shrink away. To fold into a small invisible thing that had no detectable smell. No breath. No flesh. No sound." (p. 79)

8. "The men lined up, facing us…. My brother…saw me. We were shy strangers separated by an abyss of Nazis with rifles and dogs." (p. 90)

9. "A sick stench of burning cut through the icy air. It seemed to curl around the corners of the long barracks…. It was then that I realized that the dreaded Auschwitz was empty." (p. 101)

10. "There was something triumphant in knowing. It was the never knowing that made us into helpless lumps." (p. 102)

11. "Somewhere…my brother and I had been forced to leave ourselves. Anchored in numbness, our bodies were nothing but two hungry, itching lumps." (pp. 110-111)

12. "Who our rescuers were I didn't know. But the passing through the gates of the camp was dazzling. I felt as if we were walking in a halo of light." (p. 117)

Sweden

13. "I found a big book. Reading it...the words in my new language were like so many sleeping beauties, capturing behind layers of brambles and thorns. Gradually they began to come forward, detaching from their thorny underbrush. Shedding their moss." (p. 132)

14. "I wished I had been a doll or a puppet. I wished someone would come and bend my arms and legs into the right angles so that I knew how to fit myself properly into the seat of the beautiful chair I had been asked to occupy." (p. 143)

15. "In this sadly ceremonious little room in a stone house in the middle of a rocky coastal landscape, I could not really imagine that 'mother' and 'father' were anything but two more official words." (p. 151)

16. "I was almost as tall as this new older man, whom I had known when I was so little, as my tatuœ.... In his tentative embrace I felt the strangeness of the much larger volume of daughter I had become in seven years of separation." (p. 159)

17. "I could not understand why it was not enough for [my father] just to have survived and to have his wife and children back. And to be alive in a country where there was plenty of food and where people were quietly helpful to strangers and the hating of Jews was not their main purpose in life." (p. 166)

18. "Being so clumsy at sports, and such a good girl in the classroom, distanced me from my classmates. Not many kids came forward to be my friends. And I continued to be singled out as a stranger." (p. 170)

19. "My brush dipped and caressed and tickled and wandered within my penciled out-lines. I felt as if I were a little insect, a fly or a spider, taking a slow, careful walk up and down along the strips, trailing, judging, matching and translating the quiet pale colors of the chair in the print to the chair in my drawing." (p. 175)

20. "When I looked at paintings...I was not content to remain an admirer. I became the hungry wanderer and intruder into the outlines of lace on a wrist, into eyes and noses and hair, a traveler among trees and mountains against cloudy skies, a chiseler of shapes of flower petals and out of the human body. I was a conspirator and a thief. I was an artist." (p. 176)

No Pretty Pictures: A Child of War
by Anita Lobel

Activity: Literature Extensions

After students have read the book, teachers can use the following activities to help the them extend and reinforce their learning.

Geography/History Extension

Using a large wall map of Europe, ask students to find and mark with a small "flag" (such as a pin or a toothpick) many places listed in the book. Then, using books and/or the Internet, read more about these places and learn what actually happened in these various locations.

Museum Extension

Ask whether any students have visited the Holocaust Museum in Washington, DC, or the one in Los Angeles. Ask those students who have to describe the museums. Use the Internet or other resources to find out more about these museums that are dedicated to preserving the history of the Holocaust. Look on their websites to see if they have any free materials to send to classrooms. Check to see if there are videos or audio interviews of survivors. Ask the students to discuss why preserving these painful memories is important.

Research Extension

About 1.2 million children were murdered by the Nazis during the Holocaust. Many other children were orphaned or separated from their families and never reunited. Some of them were so young when the war started that they didn't know even basic information about themselves, such as what their real names were, when their birthdays were, and where they were born. Most of these children either managed to escape or were sent to other countries after the war was over. Have students do some research about what happened to these orphaned or lost children after the war. Where did they go? Who took care of them? Where did they ultimately end up? There are many websites with photographs of these children. Students can also discuss what it would be like to not know your name or your birthday or who your parents are. How do you think this might affect you in your life?

Chapter 5
Additional Books with Corresponding Activities

> *Reading about others' misfortunes and missteps, as well as victories, and reflecting on them in meaningful ways encourages reason and resilience at a time when a strong sense of self is still developing.*
> ~Nancy Fordham & Alexa Sandman

This chapter contains two additional trade books with corresponding activities that teachers can use to differentiate instruction in the regular classroom. For the first book, *Walk Two Moons*, the primary focus of instruction centers around literature circles. The concept of literature circles is described, and a detailed list of discussion questions and extension activities for use in the circles is included. This is an excellent way to get students working with others of similar ability on projects that are interesting and challenging—all of which create the perfect recipe for stimulating advanced readers to stretch themselves in an enjoyable way.

The second book, *The Schernoff Discoveries*, is the only book of the four that utilizes humor throughout to highlight the ways in which gifted middle school students try to fit in while also demonstrating their unique identities, which sometimes simply can't be hidden. Although laughably funny in many places, this book also contains some serious messages about important themes like friendship and courage. Gifted adolescents will identify with the main character of this book on several levels, with the added bonus of enjoying themselves tremendously as they read it.

Walk Two Moons

by Sharon Creech

Summary

This is the story of a 13-year-old girl named Salamanca who learns of life's lessons while taking a car trip from Ohio to Idaho with her eccentric grandparents. While they are driving, Salamanca tells her grandparents the story of her friend Phoebe, whose mother disappeared. Interwoven with this story is Sal's story about her own mother, who left one day and never returned—a fact which Sal has great trouble accepting.

A winner of the 1995 Newbery Medal, this is a book that is both humorous and touching, with an element of mystery as well. Adolescent gifted readers will appreciate the poignancy of the story that Sal tells her grandparents, as well as Sal's own story of making peace with her missing mother. This book facilitates discussions about:

- Needing to understand
- Accepting difficult truths
- Empathy
- Facing identity issues
- Feeling different
- Learning about relationships with others
- Moral concerns
- Sensitivity

Walk Two Moons
by Sharon Creech

Vocabulary Words

The following vocabulary words are found in the book *Walk Two Moons*.

caboodle	mussed	wail
peculiar	ambush	gorged
walloping	pandemonium	rubbish
peculiarity	cinch	descended
ornery	shrapnel	chaotic
devour	gullible	unadulterated
parched	intriguing	impulse
dignified	bashed	sarcastic
lunatic	rummaging	slouch
defiance	elaborate	besieging
gnarled	quarry	quivering
omnipotent	malevolent	persuasion
cadaver	puttering	shebang
scads	prodding	careening
ruination	gouged	eerie
gallantly	notion	somberly
damsel	flailed	horrid
distress	prowled	shivery
diabolic	colossal	pious
divulge	cavorted	berserk
muesli	malinger	ogling
primly	console	quizzical
hankering	farfetched	dissuade
lunacy	tottered	nuzzled

Walk Two Moons
by Sharon Creech

Activity: Developing Vocabulary

Explain to students that they will be completing an assignment that involves vocabulary words found in the book they are about to read. Then discuss word categories with them. Group the students into pairs, and give them the vocabulary list for this book. Ask the groups to choose six words from the list that they don't already know, and have them create categories for those words. In order to create appropriate categories, the students must know the definition of each of their words. They will need to use dictionaries or computers to locate these definitions, as well as to group the words into categories. Some students may create categories based simply on word endings or whether the word is a noun or an adjective. This is okay. However, some students will go deeper by looking at the meanings of the words to create categories. Still others may create categories using word origins. They can create charts like the one that follows here.

Word	Definition	Category

When the students have completed their assignment, the groups can volunteer to share their words, definitions, and categories with the class so that others can learn from them. When a group finishes its presentation of the words and categories, the members put their chart up on the board for all to see. The teacher can then ask if any other group may have chosen some of the same words, and if so, if they chose the same category for it. It can be enlightening for students to see that words can fit into more than one category.

This sharing of words, definitions, and categories can be spread out over the course of a week—10 minutes or so each day, perhaps. Eventually, all or most of the words should get some mention. After a week, if some words have still not been defined, the teacher can cover the definitions in another way, possibly by assigning a word to each group that volunteers.

A Note of Caution: If the teacher offers a word category as an example at the beginning of this assignment, the students will often follow that lead and can lose sight of their own original thoughts. However, this does not mean that teachers can't hold a discussion before completing the activity about different ways in which words can be categorized. They just need to be sure to let the students form their own ideas.

Walk Two Moons
by Sharon Creech

Activity: Literary Elements

Sharon Creech uses language masterfully in this book. She also utilizes literary elements that gifted readers will appreciate. Once they fully understand and can recognize these elements, they can begin using them in their own writing.

Metaphors and Similes:

Discuss the use of metaphoric language and how authors often use this method for giving readers a better sense of the events in the book. This type of writing allows readers to "feel" words by attaching them to other recognizable ideas. Examples of metaphors include phrases such as "He has the heart of a lion" or "She cried great rivers from her eyes." Examples of similes are "She was as pale as a ghost" or "He was as quick as lightning."

Symbolism:

There is much symbolism in this book. Talk about ways in which authors use symbolism to give readers a deeper understanding in the story. Examples are a bouquet of red roses symbolizing love and an owl symbolizing wisdom.

Ask students to record metaphors, similes, and examples of symbolism that they find throughout the book in their literature journals. Be sure to have them include page numbers. After everyone has read the book, the students can compare and contrast what they found, along with their opinions of which metaphors and similes they particularly liked and what symbolism they found most important to the meaning of the book.

Examples of Metaphors and Similes	Examples of Symbolism
Page #:	Page #:
Page #:	Page #:
Page #:	Page #:
Page #:	Page #:
Page #:	Page #:

Walk Two Moons
by Sharon Creech

Activity: Literature Circles

It is important for gifted readers to have opportunities to discuss the books they read. They will deepen their experience of the literature and broaden their understanding of it if they can talk with others about literary themes and elements, as well as their thoughts and opinions about the stories. Literature circles are a good way to do this. The following information and activities will help middle school English teachers implement literature circles. Teachers should feel free to modify the activities to meet specific timelines or individual needs of their gifted readers.

To create literature circles, teachers should:

1. Group students by ability so that gifted readers can work with academic peers.

2. Discuss the rules for working in a group, highlighting the importance of making sure that everyone is able to participate and allowing all members to feel that they can share their views without criticism.

3. Instruct the students on the different roles that students play in the groups. These roles can include the discussion leader, vocabulary finder, recorder, questioner, observer, and time keeper. Teachers can make up new roles as needed.

4. Remember to train the students to brainstorm, to express ideas freely, to learn that many of the discussion prompts will not have right or wrong answers, and to understand that it is okay to explore a variety of different viewpoints.

5. Model ways to ask and answer questions so that students can practice those methods of communication when they are in their groups.

6. Select discussion formats. When and how often will the groups meet? What are the goals for the groups, and how will members meet those goals?

The literature circle activities and materials provided in the pages that follow for *Walk Two Moons* have been chosen based on questioning strategies developed with the use of Bloom's Taxonomy of Thinking. Teachers can use these questions to differentiate the content for each group's ability level. While all students will have the opportunity to work within literature circles, not all students will receive the same activities. Some activities will be more challenging than others.

The chart that follows is an example of a schedule for working in literature circles to read and discuss Sharon Creech's *Walk Two Moons*. Remember that literature circles should not be considered the entire reading program for an English class. They should be used as a strategy to differentiate instruction in mixed-ability classrooms and to help integrate activities into the curriculum that appeal to the different ways in which students learn. This sample calendar demonstrates using literature circles on alternating days; the other days are devoted to the teaching of regular English department requirements.

Sample Planning Chart for Literature Circles for *Walk Two Moons*

Week 1				
MON	**TUES**	**WED**	**THURS**	**FRI**
Begin the Process Explain literature circles to the class. Group students based on their ability levels in reading. Complete the vocabulary activity, and introduce the book to be read.	Regular English program requirements	**Introduce the Book to the Class** Read the quote: *"Don't judge a man until you walk two moons in his moccasins."* Discuss possible meanings and interpretations. Students write their responses in their response journals. Assign Chapters 1-10 to be read before the first literature circle meeting.	Regular English program requirements	Regular English program requirements

Week 2				
Meeting #1: The groups meet to decide upon roles that each member will assume to accomplish given tasks. Discuss Chapters 1-10, and complete the assignments for this meeting. (*Sample assignments can be found on the following pages.*) Read Chapters 11-15 for the next meeting.	Regular English program requirements	**Meeting #2:** The groups meet to discuss Chapters 11-15. The *vocabulary finder* introduces a mystery word, and the group discusses the importance of that word to themes in the book. The group also uses discussion prompts provided by the teacher to talk about other elements of the book. (*Discussion prompts can be found on the following pages.*) The *recorder* takes notes on the group's thoughts and feelings about the prompts. Read Chapters 16-25 for the next meeting.	Regular English program requirements	Regular English program requirements

MON	TUES	WED	THURS	FRI
Week 3				
Meeting #3: Students in each group begin the meeting by reviewing notes from the previous meeting. They also make changes to their style of meeting, if necessary. The *vocabulary finder* introduces another mystery word, and the *questioner* reads the question for the group to discuss and take notes on. Discussion prompts are provided. Read Chapters 26-31 for the next meeting.	Regular English program requirements	**Meeting #4:** The students get into their groups and begin their collaboration and discussion about the book. Members ask questions, as well as interpret text read for the assignment. The members begin thinking about a group project to present the book to the class. Read Chapters 32-37 for next meeting.	Regular English program requirements	**Meeting #5:** The groups meet and follow the same format as before. Students use discussion prompts as assigned by the teacher. Read Chapters 38-44 for the next meeting.
Week 4				
Meeting #6: Students have now finished reading the book. Group members continue performing roles and responsibilities. They engage in reflective dialogue relating to the book and complete assignments given to them by the teacher. Group members also choose a project to complete that demonstrates their understanding of the story and provides an analysis of the book.	Regular English program requirements	**Meeting #7:** The groups meet to accomplish several tasks. Members will complete evaluation forms about their experience of working in a group. They will also fill out self-evaluation forms about how they feel they performed in the group dynamic. The groups will spend time completing their final projects, as well as working on presentation skills.	Regular English program requirements	**Group Presentations** Each group will present its final project and discuss the students' interpretations of the book. Members will also answer questions from the class. The teacher will provide feedback and collect the final projects for assessment purposes.

Walk Two Moons

by Sharon Creech

Activity: Discussion Questions and Prompts for Literature Circles

The following questions and prompts are optimal for use in literature circles. They vary in level of difficulty so that they can be used with groups of different ability levels. Some of the questions are from the knowledge, comprehension, and application levels of Bloom's Taxonomy of Thinking. These should be used with students who need reinforcement in these more basic areas. Other questions have been written to challenge advanced readers. These questions require gifted readers to judge, analyze, synthesize, and evaluate information. All of the questions are followed by the thinking levels they require under Bloom's Taxonomy so that teachers can easily identify and select which questions they would like to use to challenge their advanced readers.

Please do not attempt to use all of the questions—it would be overwhelming to the students. Pick and choose questions that will meet the needs of the members of each group. Depending on the makeup of the classroom, the number of questions assigned may differ from group to group. Each of the groups can share their responses with the class as a whole, if it seems appropriate.

Chapters 1–10

1. At the end of Chapter 1, Sal describes her father chipping away at the plaster wall as they waited for her mother to return. She says that this reminds her of her friend Phoebe's story, and Sal relates her own story to that of Phoebe's. Why do you think the author layered one story on top of another in this book? Evaluate the purpose of layering stories upon stories. (*evaluation*)

2. In Chapter 2, Sal explains that her trip with her grandparents has many purposes, but she also says, "The real reasons were buried beneath piles and piles of unsaid things" (p. 5). What do you think Sal means by this? (*analysis, synthesis*)

3. "Salamanca Tree Hiddle" is a very unusual name. Explain how Sal's parents chose her name. (*knowledge*)

4. Sal begins to tell the story of Phoebe in Chapter 3 while traveling in the car with her grandparents. Phoebe approaches Sal during lunch and tells Sal that she thinks Sal is courageous. Sal says, "What I have since realized is that if people expect you to be brave, sometimes you pretend that you are, even when you are frightened right down to your very bones" (p. 14). Do you agree with this statement? Why or why not? Do some people pretend to be brave when in fact they are not? What is your opinion regarding this type of behavior? (*application, evaluation*)

5. The reader gets to meet Mrs. Cadaver's mother, Mrs. Partridge, in Chapter 4. Find the quote in this chapter in which Phoebe compares herself with Mrs. Partridge. What do you think Phoebe means? How is she alike or different from Mrs. Partridge? (*knowledge, comprehension, analysis, synthesis*)

6. Chapter 5 brings the story from the past to the present. Readers are now listening to Sal talk about her car trip to Idaho, and we learn about Sal's grandparents. They have some very peculiar behaviors. In one scene, Gramps helps a woman who is having car trouble. Why would the author include this scene in the story? (*comprehension, application, analysis*)

7. Reflecting upon these first chapters, describe the relationship that Sal has with her father, with her grandparents, and with Phoebe. (*knowledge, comprehension, application*)

8. Chapter 6 reveals more about Phoebe's family. Sal has dinner with the family and discovers something interesting about Phoebe's mother: When Mrs. Winterbottom talks, no one seems to listen. Sal comments, "…the main impression I got was that she was used to being plain and ordinary, that she was not supposed to do anything too shocking" (p. 31). We learned a little bit about Sal's own mother earlier in the book. Using what you have learned about Sal's mother so far, compare and contrast these two mothers. How are they alike or different? Explain your answer. (*knowledge, comprehension, analysis, synthesis*)

9. There is an element of mystery in this story. Explain what Phoebe believes happened to Mr. Cadaver. Evaluate her opinion regarding the Cadaver family. (*knowledge, comprehension, synthesis, evaluation*)

10. In Chapter 7, Sal provides information about her relationship with her mother: "When my mother had been there, I was like a mirror. If she was happy, I was happy. If she was sad, I was sad" (p. 38). So when Sal's mother left, Sal wasn't sure how to feel. After a while, however, Sal discovers that she feels happy. "I said to myself, 'Salamanca Tree Hiddle, you can be happy without her'" (pp. 38-39). What does this tell you about Sal? Why does this thought make her feel sorry? (*analysis, synthesis, evaluation*)

11. Sal keeps hearing the words: "*rush, hurry, rush.*" Judge the meaning of these whispers. Make a prediction for why these words keep coming to Sal's mind. (*analysis, synthesis*)

12. Chapter 7 ends with Sal telling the reader that she and her grandparents are traveling the same path that her mother had taken when she went to Idaho. Why would her grandparents decide to travel this route? (*analysis, synthesis*)

13. Chapter 8 brings a new character to the story. A stranger appears at the Winterbottom house and asks to see Mrs. Winterbottom, but she is not there at the time. Determine the importance of this stranger. If you were home with a friend in a situation like this, would you open the door? Justify your answer. How do you predict that this new character might influence or change the story? (*application, analysis, synthesis*)

14. Chapter 9 provides more details about the Winterbottom family. Phoebe tells her mother about the stranger who knocked on the door. Her mother becomes upset and instructs Phoebe not to tell her father. Phoebe is confused and says, "Usually my mother tells my father absolutely everything" (p. 50). Do you think this statement is true? Why or why not? What do you think about the unusual behavior exhibited by Phoebe's mother? (*knowledge, comprehension, application*)

15. Chapter 9 also introduces a new twist to the story. The girls find an envelope on the front porch of the Winterbottom home. The envelope contains a message: "*Don't judge a man until you've walked two moons in his moccasins.*" Determine the meaning of this quote by discussing it among the group. Record responses from the group members, and then make a guess as to why someone would leave this mysterious note on the front porch. Do you think the person who left the note was a stranger? Who do you think the note was meant for? (*comprehension, application, analysis*)

16. Chapter 10 brings readers back to the present story, in which Sal is traveling with her grandparents. Based on information from the story thus far, judge for yourself the whereabouts of Sal's mother. Where do you believe she is? Do you think she is alive or dead? What do you think has happened to her? Find evidence in what you have read so far to support your beliefs. (*comprehension, application, analysis*)

17. In order to judge or make assumptions about characters in books, we need to identify traits that these characters possess. At this point in the story, you know quite a lot about Sal. In your group, brainstorm a list of characteristics that help to define her. Do you believe she is brave, wise, weird...? Develop your list, and then choose five characteristics that you all agree are the most prominent in Sal's character. Participating in this type of dialog is tricky. If you have strong feelings about certain characteristics, then you need to defend your opinion using examples of behaviors and actions that Sal displays in the story. In other words, you need to convince other team members that your choices for character traits are the best. Good luck! (*knowledge, comprehension, application, analysis*)

Chapters 11–15

18. Chapter 11 brings another mysterious note to the Winterbottom home. This time the message reads: "*Everyone has his own agenda.*" Analyze this quote, not only for its relationship to the book, but for its relevance in our school community and in our society. Do you agree with the quote? Do you believe that this quote says something about the way in which we live? Defend your answer. (*comprehension, application, analysis*)

19. Ben seems to like Sal, but she flinches when he touches her. He comments on this, assuming that her flinching is because she isn't used to being touched by her family. This bothers Sal. Why do you think it bothers her? Why do you think she flinches when Ben touches her? (*analysis, synthesis*)

20. Describe the story of the "marriage bed," from Chapter 12, as it relates to Sal's grandparents. Why do you think the author chose to include the marriage bed story in the book? (*knowledge, application, analysis, synthesis*)

21. Chapter 12 also shows Sal and her grandparents smoking a peace pipe with an American Indian. After Sal takes a puff, a small bit of smoke curls out of her mouth, and she suddenly finds herself thinking, "There goes your mother" (p. 74). Judge the significance of this thought. What does it mean to Sal? Why would she think this? (*comprehension, application, analysis, synthesis*)

22. In Chapter 13, Sal goes back to school, and we learn about her teacher, Mr. Birkway. Many of the students are embarrassed and worried to learn that Mr. Birkway is going read their journals. Do you feel it was fair for Mr. Birkway to read the journals without telling the class ahead of time? Why or why not? If you were a student in Mr. Birkway's class, how would you have reacted? (*application, analysis*)

23. Chapter 14 talks about Sal's observations regarding her father's behavior and emotions. She notices that her dad acts differently when he is at Mrs. Cadaver's house. He seems happy when he is there visiting. When he is home, he is often sad and quiet. Discuss possible reasons for these differences in his behavior. (*application, analysis*)

24. Chapter 14 also exposes more information about Phoebe's mother. She asks Phoebe's sister, "Do you think I lead a tiny life?" (p. 88). Phoebe's sister ignores her. Why do you think the author included this scene in the book? What does it tell you about Mrs. Winterbottom? (*comprehension, application, analysis*)

25. Watching Phoebe's family ignore Mrs. Winterbottom makes Sal think about her own mother, and she questions whether there were things about her mother that she hadn't been able to see. This is the second time that Sal has had such thoughts. Why do you think Sal worries about this? Do you think that she blames herself for her mother leaving? Why or why not? (*analysis, synthesis, evaluation*)

26. In Chapter 15, Sal tells us that her mother cut her hair right before she left. Sal saves the hair and puts it, along with the postcards her mother sent her, beneath the floorboards of her room. However, she did not bring these things with her when she and her father moved. Why do you think Sal's mother cut her hair? And why didn't Sal bring it with her when she moved? Why did she leave these mementos of her mother at the farm? (*analysis, synthesis*)

27. Chapter 15 also describes how Sal and her grandparents decide to stop and take a cool plunge in a river. All three are swimming in their underwear when a teenage boy shows up on the river bank. He finds Gramps' wallet and starts to look through it. Just at that moment, Gram holds up a snake and tells everyone it just bit her on the leg. Gramps takes the boy's knife and cuts Gram's leg where she was bitten, and the boy sucks the poison out of the wound. They take Gram to the hospital, and the boy goes along. This is an important part of the story because it reveals strengths and weaknesses in some of the characters. What do you think these strengths and weaknesses are? What do you believe the boy would have done if Gram had not been bitten by the snake? Why did this boy go to the hospital with them, and why did he choose to not take the $50.00 Gramps offered him for helping them? (*comprehension, application, analysis*)

28. Cutting the skin where a snake has bitten it and sucking poison out of the wound is no longer considered good advice for treating a snakebite. Do some research and find out what doctors now recommend if someone is bitten by a snake. (*application*)

Chapters 16-25

29. In Chapter 16, Sal reflects upon the "singing tree" that was on their farm. When she stood beneath it, she heard a true birdsong coming from its branches. After she found out that her mother would not be returning home, she climbed the tree next to the singing tree and listened all day. She and her grandparents even slept under the singing tree all night, but they didn't hear any singing. When the three leave the hospital after Gram's snakebite incident, they hear a familiar birdsong coming from a tree rimming the hospital parking lot. Gram says, "Oh, it's a good sign, don't you think?" (p. 100). What does Gram mean by this? Is there any connection between Sal's mother and Gram's statement about hearing what she interprets as a good sign? (*application, analysis, synthesis*)

30. Sal continues to hear the whispers, but they have changed. The whispers now say, "*slow down, slow down.*" In your opinion, why have the whispers changed? List some evidence for your opinion. (*knowledge, comprehension, analysis, synthesis*)

31. In Chapter 17, another mysterious note appears on the front porch of the Winterbottom home. This time the message reads, "*In the course of a lifetime, what does it matter?*" Predict who you think is leaving these messages. Do you believe it is the strange young man who came looking for Mrs. Winterbottom? Or someone else? Explain your answer. (*application, analysis*)

32. In your group, discuss things that you think matter in a lifetime and things that probably do not matter over the course of a lifetime. What things in the book matter in a lifetime, and what things probably do not? Remember to defend your answers, as other team members may have different opinions. (*application, analysis, synthesis, evaluation*)

33. Sal explains in Chapter 18 about how her father told her they had to leave the farm in order to learn about bravery and courage. This comment seems to contradict other portions of the story. Readers first believe that Sal and her father leave the farm to escape the past and that they are not being brave in facing challenges. Now, Sal's dad tells her they will learn to be brave and courageous when they leave the farm. Compare and contrast these two viewpoints. (*analysis, synthesis, evaluation*)

34. In Chapter 19, Sal's father tells her that she is trying to catch fish in the air. Why does he tell her this? What does he mean by this statement? (*comprehension, analysis, synthesis*)

35. Chapter 20 begins with Sal recalling the story of how her mother kissed her favorite tree. Sal admits to kissing many trees after that. Why do you think Sal kissed the trees? And why do you think she tasted blackberries each time? What would cause her to experience this taste? (*analysis, synthesis*)

36. Later in this chapter, the Winterbottoms discover that their mother has left their home without explanation. This causes alarm for Phoebe and her sister. Where do you think Mrs. Winterbottom has gone? Do you think she'll return? Why do you think she left? How does this event turn the story in a new direction? (*application, analysis, synthesis*)

37. Back at school, in Chapter 21, Mr. Birkway gives an assignment to the class. He tells the students to draw their soul in 15 seconds. Most of the students draw hearts or circles or similar shapes, but two students draw the same design. Who are these students, and what did they draw? (*knowledge*)

38. In Chapter 22, Sal compares her emotions and actions when her mother left to Phoebe's reactions at her own mother leaving. Is there anything that Sal could tell Phoebe to help Phoebe deal with this issue at this point in the story? Or does Phoebe need to experience her feelings for herself, without advice? Defend your answer. (*application, evaluation*)

39. In Chapter 23, Sal tells a story about how she fell out of a tree, and her mother, who was pregnant, carried her home. That night, Sal's mother went into labor and gave birth to a dead child—a stillbirth. For the first time, the reader is able to glimpse reasons for Sal's mother's departure. Based on what you know now, why do you think Sal's mother left? What is your opinion about her leaving? (*analysis, synthesis, evaluation*)

40. Compare and contrast your understanding about why Sal's mother left with why you think Phoebe's mother left. (*comprehension, application*)

41. Phoebe finds another message on her front porch in Chapter 24. This time the message says, "*You can't keep the birds of sadness from flying over your head, but you can keep them from nesting in your hair.*" What does this message mean, and how is it significant to the story thus far? Think about all of the events leading up to this message. Can you relate this message to the events in the story? (*comprehension, application, analysis, synthesis*)

42. In Chapter 25, Phoebe and Sal go to their friend Mary Lou's house for dinner, and Phoebe makes a scene at the dinner table about not being able to eat anything that has been prepared for the meal. Why do you think Phoebe does this? What causes her to be so critical and so controlling? How would you have acted if you had been Mary Lou's parents? (*analysis, synthesis, evaluation*)

Chapters 26–31

43. At the end of Chapter 26, Sal dreams of her mother climbing a ladder, going up and up and up. What is the significance of this dream? (*comprehension, application*)

44. In Chapter 27, Mrs. Cadaver writes a note to Phoebe telling her that her mother is okay. How does Phoebe react to this message? In your opinion, why does Phoebe react this way? Why do you think Phoebe's mother contacted Mrs. Cadaver and not someone from her own family? (*knowledge, comprehension, application, analysis, synthesis*)

45. As Sal continues telling her story about Phoebe to her grandparents, she says that she had wanted to explain to Phoebe that maybe Phoebe's mother left for reasons that had nothing to do with Phoebe. Her grandparents' reaction to this statement leads Sal to a sudden realization. What is it? How do you think this will affect Sal for the rest of the story? (*knowledge, comprehension, application*)

46. Sal and her grandparents arrive in the Black Hills of South Dakota in Chapter 28. The whispers have changed again. Sal now hears "*rush, hurry, hurry*" again. Why do the whispers keep changing? What is the author's purpose for telling readers that the whispers are changing? (*comprehension, analysis*)

47. Chapter 29 shows Sal debating with others in her class about how awful death is. Ben responds by saying, "Maybe dying could be normal *and* terrible" (p. 183). Do you agree with this? Can something be both terrible and normal at the same time? How does this apply to Sal's situation? To Phoebe's? (*application, analysis, synthesis, evaluation*)

48. Mrs. Partridge is a blind woman who lives with Mrs. Cadaver. She seems to know a lot without being able to see. Define the role that Mrs. Partridge plays in the book. Predict how her influence will be felt throughout the rest of the storyline. (*application, synthesis*)

49. In Chapter 30, Sal goes into great detail telling the reader about a sort of ritual that she performs to remember her mother. She says, "This was not a game. It was a necessary, crucial thing to do. If I did not have these things and remember these occasions, then she might disappear forever. She might never have been" (p. 196). What does Sal mean by this? Why would her mother disappear forever? How could she have never existed? Analyze what Sal is really saying here. (*comprehension, analysis, synthesis*)

50. By the end of Chapter 30, readers know a lot about both Phoebe's family and Sal's family. Compare and contrast these two families. Tell how they are alike and how they are different. Think about the events that changed each family, as well as how the members of each family reacted to these events. (*knowledge, comprehension, analysis, synthesis*)

51. Phoebe finds another message on her front porch in Chapter 31. This time the message says, "*We never know the worth of water until the well is dry.*" What is the meaning of this message, and why is it significant at this point in the story? Who do you believe is leaving the messages? (*comprehension, application, analysis, synthesis*)

52. In Chapter 31, Sal and Phoebe go to the police station for a second time to talk to the police about Mrs. Winterbottom's "kidnapping." While they are there, Sal sees something on the desk of one of the police officers. What does Sal see, and how does this information change your opinion of the strange young man who appeared on the porch of the Winterbottom home? (*knowledge, comprehension, application*)

Chapters 32–31

53. In Chapter 32, Sal tells us that she prays to a tree outside. This is not the first time she has talked about praying to trees. Why do you suppose she does this? Does it have anything to do with her mother? Does it have anything to do with her story of kissing trees? What about with her name and her mother's name? What do trees symbolize for Sal? (*analysis, synthesis, evaluation*)

54. The author finally begins putting together some pieces of the puzzle in Chapter 32. We learn that Mr. Birkway is the twin brother of Mrs. Cadaver, and Mrs. Partridge is the mother of both Mrs. Cadaver and Mr. Birkway. In what ways does knowing about these relationships change Sal's opinion of each of these characters? (*knowledge, comprehension*)

55. In Chapter 33, Sal and Phoebe learn that Mrs. Cadaver's husband died in a car accident and that Mrs. Cadaver was a nurse in the emergency room when the accident happened. That night, Sal thinks about everything that Mrs. Cadaver must have gone through when she realized that two of the patients coming in to the emergency room were her own husband and mother. As these thoughts run through her head, Sal says, "I started wondering if the birds of sadness had built their nest in Mrs. Cadaver's hair…. Her husband dying and her mother being blinded were events that *would* matter in the course of a lifetime. I saw everyone else going on with their own agendas while Mrs. Cadaver was frantically trying to keep her husband and her mother alive. Did she regret anything? Did she know the worth of water before the well was dry? All those messages had invaded my brain and affected the way I looked at things" (pp. 220-221). Sal now truly understands the messages left on Phoebe's front porch. She also seems to be learning and accepting things that she did not want to accept before. Explain how Sal is growing and changing since the beginning of the story. (*knowledge, comprehension*)

56. The story shifts back to the travelers in Chapter 34 as they go to Yellowstone National Park to see the famous geyser Old Faithful. Gram crawls under the rope to get closer. Why do you think she so desperately wanted to see Old Faithful? (*comprehension, analysis, synthesis*)

57. Chapter 35 shows Sal calling Sergeant Bickle and pretending to be someone else to get information about his son. What is your opinion of this action? Is Sal wrong to do this? Why or why not? (*analysis, synthesis, evaluation*)

58. Sal and Phoebe finally find Phoebe's mother in Chapter 36. Predict what Mrs. Winterbottom will say when she explains the reason for her leaving. Who do you think the "lunatic" is now? (*application, analysis, synthesis*)

59. Sal goes to the hospital and finds Ben and his mother. She says that she had a hunch Ben's mother would be there. Why would she think this? Use details from the story to back up your answer. (*comprehension, application*)

Chapters 38-44

60. Phoebe describes how she watched her mother and the "lunatic" in Chapter 38, and she is angry about seeing them together. Why do you think she feels this way? (*comprehension*)

61. Readers learn in Chapter 39 that Mrs. Winterbottom had another son named Mike that the family didn't know about. Mike was the stranger who showed up at their door. How does this information affect the Winterbottom family? Readers also learn the

identity of the person who was leaving the messages on the porch. Tell who was leaving the messages and why. (*knowledge, comprehension*)

62. Why do you suppose Phoebe's mother came back looking completely different than Sal had ever seen her—"magnificent," in Sal's opinion. She had even cut her hair. Sal's mother had also cut her hair right before she left. What do you think this kind of change in outside appearance signified to each of these women? (*application, analysis, synthesis*)

63. In Chapter 40, Sal goes to talk with Mrs. Cadaver. What is it that finally allows her to do this? Why do you think she has avoided it for so long? (*analysis, synthesis*)

64. Chapter 40 signifies the end of the story about Phoebe. In Chapter 41, readers are now in the present with Sal, who is still traveling with her grandparents. Gram becomes very ill, and they take her to a hospital. While they are there, Sal offers to sit outside with another visitor's dog. As she is doing this, she has several revelations—about the consequences of one's actions, about keeping oneself locked up, and about weaning away from one's mother. Explain why these insights are significant for Sal. (*application, analysis*)

65. Gramps stays with Gram in the hospital, but because he knows how important it is for Sal to get to her destination before it is too late, he hands her the car keys. Sal understands what she must do—she must finish the last few miles of the trip alone so that she can get to Idaho for her mother's birthday. Why do you think the author chose to have Sal face this last leg of her journey alone? Is there anything symbolic about this? If so, what is it? (*analysis, synthesis, evaluation*)

66. Sal drives the car to the site of a bus wreck on the side of a steep mountain. In Chapter 42, she parks the car and walks down to see the mangled bus. A sheriff arrives who talks to Sal and then takes her to see her mother's grave. This chapter is powerful. It describes the courage that Sal had to have in order to make the trip alone, to walk to the mangled bus in the pre-dawn light, and to go to her mother's grave with the sheriff. Sal says of her mother, "She isn't actually gone at all. She's singing in the trees" (p. 268). What does this mean, and how does it relate to the other events that occurred in the story? (*comprehension, application, analysis*)

67. The author solves another mystery in Chapter 43 by revealing that Mrs. Cadaver had been sitting next to Sal's mother on the trip and was the only person to survive the bus crash. Sal also suffers a great loss in this chapter: Gram dies in the hospital. On the night of her death, Gramps writes her a love letter. Why was it important for Gramps to write this letter to Gram? (*knowledge, comprehension, application*)

68. In the last chapter, Sal and Gramps return home, and Gram is buried on the farm. Sal and Gramps play the game they made up while coming home from Idaho. In the game, they take turns walking in someone else's moccasins. Make a list of some of the people in your life. Choose one, and talk about what it might be like to walk in that person's shoes. Describe what you learn from this experience in your journal. (*application, analysis, synthesis*)

69. In the end, Sal reflects upon the different stories that unraveled during her trip to Idaho. She says, "…just as the fireplace was behind the plaster wall and my mother's story was behind Phoebe's, I think there was a third story behind Phoebe's and my mother's, and that was about Gram and Gramps" (p. 274). Evaluate Sal's idea of a third story hiding behind her story and Phoebe's story. Do you agree with Sal that there is a third story? Explain your answer using examples from the book. (*application, analysis, synthesis*)

70. Sal realizes that her trip to Idaho was a gift from her grandparents. They were giving her a chance to walk in her mother's moccasins—to see what she had seen and feel what she might have felt on her last trip. Tell what you think was the author's purpose for including this information at the end of the book. (*comprehension, application, analysis*)

71. List the ways in which Sal grows up in the book. If you feel ambitious, you can make a chart to show how she changes. (*knowledge, comprehension, application, analysis, synthesis, evaluation*)

Walk Two Moons
by Sharon Creech

Activity: Extension Projects for Literature Circles

As groups of students work together in literature circles, they will not only discuss the story using prompts provided by the teacher, they must also decide upon a final project that will be presented to the class. Give the students the list of extension projects that appears on the following pages, and ask the groups to decide which would be the best one for them to work on. It is recommended that the groups each choose a different final project, but this can be left to the teacher's discretion. Be sure to provide time within the literature circle meetings for the groups to complete the project.

Extension Projects for *Walk Two Moons*

Directions: *Extension projects help extend your learning and allow you to demonstrate your understanding of the book. As a group, examine this list of possible projects and then decide which one your group will complete.*

Revisit, Reflect, and Recite

This project is fun for those students who enjoy participating in discussions and debates with their peers. Look at the list of questions below. As a group, choose one to discuss. First, discuss the question among yourselves. Be sure to relate your discussion to the book. Write the question and your answers on a large piece of posterboard. Your answers should included quotes and statements from the book to back them up. Cover up your answers in a fun and creative way, and then present your question to the class. The entire class will discuss possible answers. At the end of the discussion, your group will reveal your answers and the statements that support them. The piece of posterboard can then be taped to the wall or put up for display in another way.

❍ How do decisions, actions, and consequences vary depending on the different perspectives of the people involved?

❍ How is the future shaped by the past and the present?

❍ Does love require sacrifice?

❍ What is the relationship between love and trust?

Interview for a Different Perspective

The whole concept of walking two moons in another person's moccasins means that we never really understand someone until we can see things from their point of view. By the end of the book, Sal has changed her opinion of several of the adults she has known. As a group, decide who these adults are, and discuss what Sal's opinion of them was, both at the beginning of the story and at the end, once she learned more about them. Next, as an experiment to learn more about someone, your group should interview an older person. Develop a list of interview questions that you will use, and have this list approved by the teacher. Prior to the interview, your group will write a few sentences about what you know about the person. Then, conduct the interview and record what you learn. Afterword, write a few sentences about how your views of that person changed based upon what he or she told you during the interview. Your group will present your findings in the format of a talk show. One member of the group will play a guest on the show representing the person who was interviewed, and the rest of the members will be talk show hosts. The talk show hosts will ask the guest questions, and the guest will provide answers that were gathered from the interview. When the "show" is over, your group will discuss with the class how your views changed from what you thought of the person who was interviewed to what you thought after that person shared his or her experiences from a different perspective. Then compare this with some of the things that Sal learned from the adults around her and how her opinions of them evolved.

Webbing Characters and Traits

We can learn more about the characters in a book by examining how they deal with challenges in the story. Make a semantic map that identifies four types of challenges faced by the characters. Then add to the web by identifying some specific challenges for each category.

After constructing the semantic map, your group will write a summary of how each of the characters overcame these challenges (if in fact they did). In the end, choose the one trait that most of the characters portrayed in order to overcome the challenges. Discuss your findings with the class. Be prepared to defend your choice if other students in the class disagree with you.

Create a Brochure

Sal visits many places on her trip across the country with her grandparents. Your group can create a travel brochure for the places that Sal visited. You may use the Internet, maps, and other resources to collect information about these various locations. Your brochure will teach others important facts about the places mentioned in the story. Then present the brochure to the class. You can even choose a group member to act as a travel agent who is trying to tell the class all about the benefits of a particular place, using the brochure as a prop and referring to it in the presentation. There are other ways that you can present your brochure as well—think of something creative!

20-Minute Presentation

Your group will create a 20-minute presentation that combines your skills of interpretation and evaluation to teach others about this book. Make sure that your group discusses the author's use of direct and indirect characterization and parallel episodes. Mention scenes that signify change or conflict found in the story, and include important quotes that you found to be powerful to the plot. It is important that you identify and analyze the effects of complex literary devices such as figurative language, flashbacks, foreshadowing, and irony. Your goal is to enhance your classmates' understanding of the story. If you need more information on these or other literary devices, you can look them up in a dictionary or on the Internet. You may choose to use PowerPoint or another means of technology to help with your presentation.

Setting the Scene

Your group must choose a scene from the book and put on a short play that recreates that scene to help the class interpret, analyze, and evaluate actions made by the characters. To help your group begin, think about different events that take place in the story that lead to personal conflicts for the characters. Decide upon a scene that will promote discussion among class members as to their opinions about the decisions, actions, and consequences of the characters in the scene. Be prepared to defend why your group chose the scene that you ultimately selected, as well as to answer questions from the class.

Mock Trial

Pretend that the sheriff who helped Sal while she was in Idaho decides to press charges because Sal was driving without a license. Your group will perform a mock trial in front of the class to prosecute Sal for breaking this law. Choose from your group which members will act as a prosecuting attorney, a defense lawyer, a judge, Sal, and Gramps. You will need to research the legal system in order to use correct terminology for court. You must include a discussion of the difficulty often associated with ethical issues in our society. Do you think Sal should be punished for driving her grandfather's car? Do you think she was justified in driving the car? What if Sal had harmed someone while she was driving? Will the defense lawyer be able to convince the judge that Sal is innocent because she was driven by her desire to find her mother? Or will the prosecuting attorney show that "wrong is wrong" and that no one should be permitted to drive a car without a license no matter the circumstances?

Private Investigation Services

Mysterious events are a large part of the plot of this story. The author was very skillful in creating mysterious situations at the beginning of the book, building suspense throughout the story with hints and clues, and then finally solving the mysteries by the end of the book. For example, for much of the story, we don't know what has happened to Sal's mother, the identity of the person leaving messages on the Winterbottom porch, who the young man is who knocks at the Winterbottoms' front door, where Phoebe's mother goes when she leaves, or the relationship between Mrs. Cadaver, Mr. Birkway, and Mrs. Partridge. Your group has been given the task of selecting one of these mysteries and tracing it from beginning to end. To begin, your group must first select which mystery you want to investigate. Then, go back in the story to see how the author introduces that mystery, gradually gives us hints about it, and then offers more and more information until we know the truth. Record each instance where the author gives the reader clues to solve the mystery. Create a timeline or a chart on a large piece of posterboard to display this information to the class. After you have presented your timeline, discuss with the class how difficult you think it was for the author to weave four or five mysteries throughout the book. (Other groups may be tracing one of the other mysteries.)

Important Character Quotes

There are many powerful quotes in this story. Your group's task is to choose the three most important quotes found in the book. This might prove to be difficult, as group members may not agree. If there is disagreement, your group must hold a discussion that convinces everyone to agree on the same three quotes. After that, your group will write out on a piece of posterboard the quotes that you chose, the page number where they are found in the book, and the significance of those quotes to the overall impact of the story. To help your group decide which quotes to choose, consider this list of questions:

- Explain why you liked the quote.

- Did the quote help you to understand the story?

- Analyze how the quote is important to the main ideas in the plot.

- Is the quote similar to one of the themes in the book?

- Does the quote allow you to connect to your own experiences?

Afterward, you will present your findings to the class. The piece of posterboard can be taped to the wall or displayed in some other way in the classroom.

In the End...

Your group has the task of writing an obituary or a eulogy for Sal's mother. Consider character traits that were referenced in the book in order to create an accurate depiction of Sal's mother and the life she led with her family. There are many places in the story that can give you the evidence you need. You may want to look at obituaries in the local newspaper to see how they are customarily written and to use as models for yours. You will read the obituary or eulogy to the class and then discuss why you chose to include in it what you did. You can also discuss what facts or opinions you may have left out of it in respect to the deceased. What important information might you leave out of an obituary, and why? Is it fair to leave information out of an obituary that might reveal negative characteristics of a person? Consider the purpose of an obituary, as well as who the obituary is really intended for. Discuss these issues with the class.

Walk Two Moons

by Sharon Creech

Literature Circle Forms

The forms on the following pages will promote the use of literature circles by helping teachers organize, implement, and assess the process. As always, these forms may be modified to meet the needs of individual teachers. Here is some information about each form.

Discussion Log

The first form is for students to fill out both before and after the literature circle meetings. It asks them to be specific about what they liked in their reading, as well as what they may not have fully understood. These are both effective prompts to get students talking during their group meetings. The third question asks students to record what they learned from the other members of their group after the discussion has taken place. When students understand that they will be required to fill out these Discussion Logs for each of their literature circle meetings, they begin consciously looking for parts of the story that are interesting to them. They also focus during the discussions on what they are learning from others, which is an excellent way to get them constructively interacting with one another.

Comment Card

This Comment Card is not a form that students or teachers fill out. Rather, it is more of a "cheat sheet" for students who may not be comfortable expressing their opinions in peer groups. This card can be copied by the teacher and passed out to the students, who can tape it to the insides of their journals, if they wish. The card offers suggestions of appropriate wording for students to use to respectfully counter the opinions of others and state their own viewpoints during group discussions.

Self-Evaluation Card

The Self-Evaluation Card allows students to analyze their own involvement in the literature circle meetings. Two simple questions ask them what they feel they did well, and what they feel they could improve upon. The questions are purposefully broad so that students can feel free to record their assessment of both their academic skills, but also the social skills that they may feel particularly proud of or that they may realize they need to work on.

Planning the Final Project

This form, which students complete once their group has decided on their final project for their literature circle, performs a double task. First, it allows students to solidify in their minds what it is that they will be doing for their final project and how they will do it. Second, it gives teachers a good idea of which students seem to be motivated to complete the project, as well as how much they seem able and willing to participate in doing it. Clues like the ones that teachers will find on this completed form will help them to assess individual students as they work in a group setting, which can be difficult.

Anecdotal Record Form for Teachers

Teachers can use this form to record anecdotal information about individual students. Writing down specific actions that they see from the students will help teachers remember the level of participation of each student, as well as how prepared each student was for the meeting, if there were comprehension problems for any of the students, etc. Having these notes available will allow teachers to more effectively assign appropriate grades to each individual student in the groups for their progress and participation.

Individual Assessment of Student Progress

Teachers often express feelings of frustration when using literature circles because it is difficult to assess individual achievement among students. The Anecdotal Record Form and the Planning the Final Project Form can certainly assist them in this process; however, the Individual Assessment of Student Progress form will be the most helpful in assigning final grades to the individual students after the literature circle group meetings are concluded. While many of the assessment criteria on this form are somewhat subjective because they are based on teacher observations of the students, the form does offer an objective grading scale, which assigns specific grades to each student. It also includes a place for teachers to write their comments about what students did well or could improve upon to raise their grade the next time.

Literature Circles
Discussion Log

Name:_____ Date:_____

Teacher:_____ Room:_____

Title/Author of Book:_____

Reading Assignment:_____

An interesting part of the story that I would like to discuss with the group: _____

_____

_____

I did not understand this part of our reading assignment: _____

_____

_____

What I learned after talking with my group: _____

_____

_____

Literature Circles
Comment Card

If I disagree with my group members, I can say:

▼ I see your point, but I believe this might be the case: _____.

▼ Excuse me, may I offer my opinion? I feel I have some information that will help us make predictions or analyze the material more effectively. _____.

▼ I agree with you, but I would like to add _____.

▼ Could you say that again? I am not sure I understand what you are saying.

▼ I disagree with you, but let me tell you why. _____.

▼ Okay, let's look at this from a different point of view. _____.

▼ It is obvious that we have different opinions. Let's try and see if there are things that we can agree upon. _____.

Literature Circles
Self-Evaluation Card

Name: _____   Date: _____

Teacher: _____   Room: _____

Title/Author of Book: _____

These are the things I did well during our group discussion today:

I think I could improve in these areas:

Literature Circles
Planning the Final Project

Name:_____ Date:_____

Title of Book:_____ Author:_____

Members in Our Group:_____ _____

_____ _____

_____ _____

After looking at the list of extension projects, your group will choose one to complete. Write a description of the project that you have chosen below, and list the resources that you think you'll need to complete it.

_____
_____
_____
_____

Record chapters or places in the book that will give you information to help your group complete the project.

_____
_____
_____
_____

Explain how this project will demonstrate the group's understanding of the book while also reflecting upon the themes and literary elements present in it.

_____
_____
_____
_____

Literature Circles
Anecdotal Record Form for Teachers

During group discussions, I observed these students engaged in conversations, asking questions about the text, making predictions, etc:

_____   _____
_____   _____
_____   _____
_____   _____

I also noted these students because they were not engaged in the discussion; they allowed other group members to assume responsibility for the assignments and discussions:

_____   _____
_____   _____
_____   _____
_____   _____

These students attempted to participate in group discussions but were not prepared to do so because they did not read the assignment:

_____   _____
_____   _____
_____   _____
_____   _____

When talking with students individually about the book, these students could not effectively discuss literary elements, literary themes, and/or other important information about the book:

_____   _____
_____   _____
_____   _____
_____   _____

Literature Circles
Individual Assessment of Student Progress

Student Name:_____ Date:_____

Grading Criteria	Points Awarded 0-5
1. Student was prepared for group meetings	
2. Student participated in group discussions, adding meaningful comments	
3. Student performed responsibilities for the role that he/she was assigned	
4. Student contributed to the learning environment by following group rules and by exhibiting cooperative behaviors	
5. Student had an equal part in the final project as it was completed	
6. Student delivered the final presentation with the group in appropriate ways as defined by the oral speaking guidelines reviewed in class	
7. Student asked for clarification when confused	
8. Student expressed thoughts, concerns, and ideas in appropriate ways	
9. Student met deadlines	
10. Student wrote in response journal when assigned to do so	

0-10 = F, 11-20 = D, 21-30 = C, 31-40 = B, 41-50 = A

Additional comments:

_____

_____

_____

The Schernoff Discoveries
by Gary Paulsen

Summary

Harold Schernoff is a middle school science whiz and a social outcast. He likes to solve problems, and he has a theory to solve just about all of them. He and his friend, the narrator in the book, experience many funny and disastrous incidents as they strive to test Harold's theories, ranging from fishing to dating to dealing with bullies. This is a humorously entertaining story with some very serious messages for gifted adolescents about the quest to be "cool" and the meanings of true friendship.

This book facilitates discussions about:

- Friendship
- Differentness
- Being socially rejected
- Drive to understand
- Overcoming challenges
- Dealing with bullies
- Courage

The Schernoff Discoveries
by Gary Paulsen

Vocabulary Words

The following vocabulary words are found in the book *The Schernoff Discoveries.*

gravitate	bygone	apparition
neophyte	etiquette	catastrophe
proximately	condescending	probable
privy	extrapolated	bedevil
pungent	proficient	creel
reeling	ganglion	ferrules
forfeit	folly	oscillation
aversion	instinctual	emitted
brawn	seething	trepidation
rudimentary	elongated	vortex
flabbergasted	imperceptibly	diminutive
snatches	pummeled	blanched
coincided	camaraderie	
immersed	stultifying	

The Schernoff Discoveries
by Gary Paulsen

Activity: Expanding Vocabulary

Directions: *Choose eight words that you don't know from the vocabulary list you were given for this book. Then, predict or guess what you think each word means. After you have written your predictions, use a dictionary to locate the actual word definitions, and write them as well. When everyone is finished, we will see whether our predictions were close and share our findings with the class.*

1. Word:_____

My prediction or guess:_____

The definition from the dictionary:_____

2. Word:_____

My prediction or guess:_____

The definition from the dictionary:_____

3. Word:_____

My prediction or guess:_____

The definition from the dictionary:_____

4. Word:_____

My prediction or guess:_____

The definition from the dictionary:_____

5. Word:_____

My prediction or guess:_____

The definition from the dictionary:_____

6. Word:_____

My prediction or guess:_____

The definition from the dictionary:_____

7. Word:_____

My prediction or guess:_____

The definition from the dictionary:_____

8. Word:_____

My prediction or guess:_____

The definition from the dictionary:_____

The Schernoff Discoveries
by Gary Paulsen

Activity: Elements of Language

Directions: *Metaphor, simile, alliteration, and irony are all examples of literary devices or elements. These kinds of elements add interest and variety to the language in all stories. As you read the book, look for literary elements and list them in the chart below, along with the page number where you found them. Then complete the chart.*

Literary Element	Example from Book	How does it help to express a point or convey a message?
	Page #:	
	Page #:	
	Page #:	
	Page #:	
	Page #:	
	Page #:	

The Schernoff Discoveries
by Gary Paulsen

Activity: Discussion Questions and Prompts

This activity contains quotes from each chapter of the book, with corresponding discussion questions. The questions vary widely in content, from asking students to dissect and examine parts of the story, to requiring students to use their knowledge of other topics and apply it to information they have learned from the book, to having students use what they learn from their reading as a springboard for coming up with new ideas, to inviting students to form opinions about the characters and use facts from the book to defend those opinions, to prompting students to examine their feelings about friendship and a sense of belonging among peers. Each question is followed by the thinking levels it requires under Bloom's Taxonomy of Thinking. This will help you select higher-level questions for your advanced students.

You will want to carefully examine the list of questions before giving the book to students to read so that you can select which ones you want to use and then decide upon the best times to introduce them. Some of the questions naturally lend themselves to whole-class or small group discussions. Others are more sensitive in nature and would be better as prompts for journal entries. Still others may be ideal for use in literature circles or Socratic seminars. Please don't give students the entire list of questions at once and ask them to respond as they read—the students do not need to answer every question, and giving them too many at once will take the fun out of their reading.

Chapter 1: On Discovering the Benefits of Electricity

At the beginning of Chapter 1, the narrator, Harold's friend, tells us the following:

On no other level were we alike, but the fact that we were outcasts meant that we gravitated toward each other like two marbles rolling toward the center of a bowl—bouncing apart now and again but generally getting closer and closer until we were friends. (p. 3)

1. Think of the image that Harold's friend uses to describe their friendship. If you dropped two marbles into a bowl, they would roll around for a while, occasionally bouncing off one another but ultimately settling to the bottom of the bowl together. How does this image relate to friendships? What would cause friends to move closer together and then bounce apart? Has this ever happened to you? Explain. (*application, analysis*)

2. Describe how you think people typically make friends at our school. What are "cliques," and why do they form among students? How do you think the presence of cliques affects both students in the clique and students outside of it? Do you think most people find it easy or difficult to form friendships? Why or why not? (*application, analysis, synthesis*)

3. What does Harold's friend mean when he says: "On no other level were we alike"? What does he mean by the word "level"? What does the word "outcasts" mean when thinking about relationships in school? Have you ever felt like an outcast? If so, where and when? Were you able to overcome these feelings, and if so, how? (*knowledge, comprehension, application*)

4. Describe how Harold attempted to make a new form of electricity in Mrs. Johnson's class. What was the outcome? How do you think this outcome contributed to Harold's reputation in the school? (*knowledge, comprehension*)

5. Harold says, "Mrs. Johnson said atoms and electrons are the power of the sun. If we could tap into it…think of it!" (p. 5). This quote sparks our minds to think about alternative energies and how scientists have worked for years trying to harness electricity through solar power. How would using solar power to create most of the world's supply of electricity affect our society? What would be the advantages? Would there be any disadvantages? Defend your answers using information you have learned from reading or viewing programs about our country's current focus on alternative sources of energy. What are some other sources of energy being developed today? (*analysis, synthesis, evaluation*)

Chapter 2: Brain over Brawn

Chapter 2 begins with this quote:

There is always a solution. For everything. Always. Sometimes it isn't pretty and takes a little longer, but there is still a solution. ~Schernoff on problems (p.10)

6. Do you agree or disagree with Harold in the quote above? Is there always a solution to every problem? Can you think of some problems that seem to have no solutions? Be prepared to defend your answers. (*application, analysis, synthesis*)

7. Harold decides to sign up for home economics class as a way to meet girls. Harold's friend is not happy about this idea, but Harold talks him into it. Because of this decision, however, the boys are teased even worse than they had been before. But they do meet girls, and they eventually even become comfortable talking with them. Was taking home economics a wise decision for these two boys? Why or why not? Is there a difference between how the other boys in school viewed this decision versus how the girls viewed it? (*analysis, synthesis, evaluation*)

8. What are some other ways that Harold and his friend could meet girls that might not cause the other students to tease them so badly? (*analysis, synthesis*)

9. Members of the football team tease and torment the two boys. To get even, Harold bakes two cakes secretly filled with chocolate laxatives for the football team to eat. The whole team gets sick and has to forfeit that night's game. What is your opinion of Harold's actions against the members of the football team? Why do you think it was so important for Harold to get revenge? Have you ever wanted to play a prank on someone or a group of people because of the way they treated you? Explain. (*comprehension, application, analysis, evaluation*)

10. Sometimes students who are not socially accepted by their peers can become very angry at the people around them. Do you know of any examples of this? How can we, as a school or as a society, help students who don't feel accepted? (*application, analysis, synthesis*)

Chapter 3: On Discovering Interpersonal Relationships

Chapter 3 begins with this quote:

It is the complete commingling of every aspect of two people. If it happens right. If not it just makes your stomach hurt. ~Harold on love (p. 23)

11. Harold's friend tries to define the word "cool" but is not able to provide a definition. What does the word "cool" mean to you? Write your definition of this word on a sheet of paper, and tell why you believe your definition is correct. On this same piece of paper, write the name of a famous person who you consider to be cool. Next, write the name of a famous person who you believe is not cool. Tell why you think these people are cool or not cool. (*comprehension, analysis*)

12. Harold asks his friend, "So how do I do it? How do I become cool?" (p. 26). If you were Harold's friend, what advice would you give him? How would you explain to people how they can become cool at school? (*application*)

13. Many people consider appearances when thinking about which people are cool. Do you believe that appearance plays a large role when deciding on who is cool and who is not? Explain your answer. (*analysis, synthesis*)

14. If you had to choose one or the other, do you believe it is more important to be cool or to get all A's on your report card? In other words, if being cool is getting in the way of earning good grades in school, should a person stop trying to be cool and just focus on grades? Why or why not? (*application, analysis, synthesis*)

15. Harold goes on a date, but it goes terribly wrong. Harold was only trying to do what he read from books that he should do. Do books always offer good advice? Do books sometimes contain bad advice? Is it possible that the advice Harold read was good, but that he only followed it incorrectly? Can people learn everything they need to know from reading? Or do some things have to be learned in other ways? (*analysis, synthesis, evaluation*)

16. Harold's friend says about the two of them: "Because Harold and I had pretty much evolved away from junior-high society, neither of us knew exactly what *normal* meant" (p. 26). What does Harold's friend mean when he makes this statement? In your opinion, what does it mean to be "normal"? Are "normal" and "cool" the same thing? Explain how these two concepts are alike and how they are different when used to describe middle school students. (*comprehension, analysis*)

17. "As it happened, there was just enough time for Harold to begin research on the subject (of dating), to 'gather sufficient data,' as he put it, which made him completely dangerous" (p. 27). What does Harold's friend mean when he says this? Why does he use the term "dangerous"? How does having only a little bit of information make someone dangerous? (*comprehension, application*)

18. As Harold is getting ready for his date, his friend describes how badly out-of-style he looks. But what he actually tells Harold is that Harold looks great. Why doesn't Harold's friend tell him the truth? Would the truth have helped Harold better prepare for his date? Why or why not? How do you think Harold would have reacted to hearing

that he "was almost beyond help" (p. 24)? Is the narrator being a good friend or a bad friend when he doesn't tell Harold the truth about Harold's appearance? (*comprehension, analysis, synthesis, evaluation*)

Chapter 4: On Discovering Gravity

Chapter 4 begins with this quote:

Velocity squared times mass equals energy—except with snow, where everything is apparently doubled. ~Harold on snow sports (p. 34)

19. Harold says to his friend, "One of the reasons we have so much trouble becoming popular and remaining popular is our lack of social standing" (p. 35). Evaluate the meaning of this quote. What does "social standing" mean to you? What happens to middle school students if they lack social standing? Do you believe this to be fair? Explain. (*comprehension, application, analysis, synthesis, evaluation*)

20. Harold tells his friend that if they learn to ski, their social standing will improve. Make a list of other ways that students can improve their social standing at school. (*comprehension, application*)

21. Right before Harold begins his ski run, his friend says, "In my heart I sought revenge but I honestly thought he would make it. He was so confident, so cleanly cool about the start that I thought, rats, he's going to do it right" (pp. 42-43). Why does his friend want Harold to fail at skiing? Explain. (*comprehension, analysis*)

Chapter 5: On Making Friends

Chapter 5 begins with this quote:

Death is easy—it's living that's hard. ~Harold on Chimmer (p. 47)

22. Harold's friend is constantly bullied by a boy named Chimmer. The bullying has been taking place for many years, and Harold's friend has arranged his life to avoid Chimmer when he can. Make a list of the ways in which Chimmer bullies Harold's friend. What are some ideas for overcoming bullies in school besides trying to avoid them? (*knowledge, comprehension, analysis, synthesis*)

23. Should there be consequences or punishments for students who go out of their way to bully other students? If so, what kind of punishment would be appropriate? (*analysis, synthesis, evaluation*)

24. In this chapter, Harold demonstrates great courage by standing up to Chimmer to make him stop bullying his friend. The result of this action changes the friend's life forever. Explain what happened. Would you have done the same thing if you had been in Harold's situation? What else could you have done to help your friend? (*knowledge, comprehension, analysis, synthesis*)

25. Harold's friend says, "I decided then that for the rest of my life I would always look for the bowling pin that would help me through the tough spots" (p. 63). What does he mean when he says this? What does the bowling pin represent? (*knowledge, comprehension, analysis*)

26. Are there any "bowling pins" that have helped you through some of the tough spots in your life? List some of them. Next, predict what types of "bowling pins" you may need in the future. (*application, synthesis, evaluation*)

Chapter 6: On Angling

Chapter 6 begins with this quote:

A fish doesn't know anything, ever, at all, about anything. Which is why fish are so hard to catch. ~Harold on fishing with worms (p. 64)

27. Harold tells his friend that he wants to learn how to fish, speculating that it ought to be simple to do. His friend protests, saying, "Harold, fishing is…is more…. It's just more." Harold replies, "Then that is what you'll teach me. All about what makes it more" (pp. 66-67). What does his friend mean when he says this? (*comprehension, analysis, synthesis*)

28. Several funny things happen to the two boys as they fish along the banks of the river. Create a series of pictures that depict some of the funny incidents that occur while Harold and his friend are fishing. Make your pictures into a comic strip. (*application, synthesis*)

29. Harold experiences a serious accident while fishing—an accident that could have killed him. Evaluate what you would have done in this situation if you were Harold's friend. Would you risk your life for your best friend? Why or why not? (*synthesis, evaluation*)

30. Harold's friend says that he has never seen Harold fail at anything except fishing. Why do you believe Harold isn't successful at fishing? Do you think his friend is correct about this? Think of the other experiments that Harold has tried. Most of them seemed to fail (for example, his experiment with electricity, dating, skiing). Why doesn't his friend consider these experiments failures? (*analysis, synthesis, evaluation*)

Chapter 7: On the Nature of Wealth

Chapter 7 begins with this quote:

A fool and his golf balls are soon parted. ~Harold on becoming rich (p. 78)

31. Throughout the book, readers are given several clues about the family life of Harold's friend. For example, he says, "Harold had a room and three meals a day, and his parents bought all of his clothes. I thought he lived in luxury" (p. 79). What does this quote tell you about Harold's friend? What kind of home life do you think he has? What in the quote supports your thoughts? Find at least three other instances in the book in which Harold's friend tells us about his home life. (*comprehension, analysis, synthesis*)

32. Through a series of scientific equations, Harold convinces his friend that they should become golf caddies at the local golf club to earn money. His friend thinks the idea is a bad one, and he says, "But Harold had a way saying things so that even when you knew they were impossible it seemed like they could happen" (p. 82). Have you ever felt this way about someone? Tell about a time when someone tried to convince you to do something that you knew would be difficult. What did this person do to convince you

that it would be possible? What happened in the end? Was it possible or not? (*application, analysis, synthesis*)

33. Harold's friend says this about Harold: "...he knew too much and knowledge can sometimes be a very frightening thing" (p. 86). What is Harold's friend trying to say about Harold? How do you know? Do you believe that this statement is true? Have you ever known anyone who had "too much knowledge?" Analyze what "too much knowledge" means as it is used here. (*application, analysis, synthesis*)

34. The boys go to the lake at night to retrieve golf balls that have sunk to the bottom of the lake so that they can earn enough money to buy a car. Would you have participated in this adventure with Harold and his friend? Why or why not? (*application, evaluation*)

35. After working hard to retrieve the golf balls from a pond, the boys end up with 672 golf balls and have been promised a dime for each one from the golf pro. The narrator recalls the costs of certain things during the time that he was a boy. For example:

   ○ A man working in a factory earned $40.00 a week
   ○ A doctor's visit cost $5.00
   ○ A hamburger cost 15 cents
   ○ A movie and popcorn each cost 10 cents
   ○ A Coke cost 5 cents
   ○ Rides at the fair cost 10 cents

   Compare these prices to how much things cost today. Why does the author include this information about the prices of everyday things? (*application, analysis, synthesis*)

36. The two boys earn $67.20 from the golf shop manager, which makes them feel rich. Although they have been working to earn money for a car, after seeing the money, Harold's friend wants to spend it on things like Pepsis and movies and hamburgers. Harold stays firm; the money is for a car. What does this conversation say about each of the boys? Does it tell you anything about their families and their home life? About their goals? Their views of the future? (*analysis, synthesis*)

37. Harold and his friend buy a 1934 Dodge sedan from an old farmer. While Harold is haggling with the farmer about the price, the farmer says, "...and that's my final offer if you want this here Dodge touring automobile." Harold agrees to the price and whispers to his friend, "I couldn't see that much for a car...but for a touring *automobile*..." (p. 94). How does a change in the wording of a thing make it seem different? Words can be very powerful. Can you think of any other things that are called by different names to make them seem better? (Think, for example, of "pre-owned" instead of "used" cars, or "service technicians" instead of "repairmen.") (*analysis, synthesis*)

38. Even though the car is clearly in very poor shape, the boys are thrilled with their purchase. Harold's friend says, "Everything had changed. We were free of the silly shackles of voice-changing, pimple-ridden, shyness-tormented youth; we had grown in stature and our own minds with the sound of her engine firing and turning over. That world was gone forever" (pp. 96-97). What does he mean by this? (*comprehension, analysis, synthesis, evaluation*)

39. Although the car was hard to drive and wouldn't go into third gear, the boys drove it several miles until, quite suddenly, the engine exploded and caught on fire. Why did the boys feel good even after the car blew up and burned completely? Would you feel the same way after losing all your money when the car blew up? Explain. (*application, analysis*)

40. Analyze the following quote by restating it in your own words: "And we started the long walk back to town, into our lives and all that would come to us" (p. 99). What does this mean? Predict what will happen next in the adventures of these two friends. Then read the Afterword to see how they turned out as adults. (*analysis, synthesis*)

The Schernoff Discoveries
by Gary Paulsen

Activity: Analyzing Quotes

Directions: *The author provides a quote at the beginning of each chapter that offers insight as to what the chapter will be about, as well as a peek into Harold's thinking. These quotes are considered the "Schernoff Discoveries." Choose two of the quotes, and use the organizer below to help you analyze and comment on these discoveries.*

	The Discovery	Evidence from the story that supports Harold's discovery	Your Analysis
Quote: From Chapter #:			
Quote: From Chapter #:			

The Schernoff Discoveries
by Gary Paulsen

Activity: Using Bloom's Taxonomy

Providing gifted readers with opportunities to reach higher levels of learning is important. While all students should be given opportunities to work at the higher levels, teachers must make sure that students are ready to work at these levels. The list below follows Bloom's Taxonomy of Thinking, beginning with the lowest levels and progressing to the highest. Each level contains questions and activities that will challenge students at that level. Teachers may choose to assign activities to students based on individual ability levels, or they may allow students to choose from the list based on individual interests. It is important, however, to make provisions for all students to experience both challenge and success.

Knowledge

❍ List two events in this story that made you think of other books you have read.

❍ Who is the author, and what other books has he written? Research this author using books or the Internet, and provide a brief description of the other books that he has written.

Comprehension

❍ Find three words in the book that describe Harold and three words that describe his friend. Look for words that depict different characteristics of the two boys.

❍ Harold's friend says, "While I remained spindly-legged, short, skinny and runty well into my first year in the army, Chimmer developed a muscular torso when he was about four" (p. 48). This is an example of exaggeration to add humor to the story. Find other instances in the book in which the narrator exaggerates to be humorous.

Application

❍ Use a large sheet of paper to create a timeline of events in the story.

❍ Create a poster that tells others about Harold. Use character traits that will help others gain a true picture of Harold in their minds. Include both Harold's strengths and his weaknesses.

Analysis

- Identify some of the themes that you found in this story. Make a list of these themes, and then match them with titles from other books. For example, what other books do you know that contain themes of friendship?

- Create a chart that compares you and Harold. How are you alike, and how are you different? How would some of your character traits help Harold in his life? Are there any character traits possessed by Harold that would help you in life?

Synthesis

- Pretend that you are friends with both boys in the story. What role would you play in this friendship? Would you try to help the boys become more socially accepted? Why or why not? What would you try to change about Harold or his friend if you were a friend to both of them? Why would this be important in middle school?

- There are many funny parts in this book. Choose a scene that you think is one of the funniest, and create a comic strip of it. Draw at least four frames for your comic strip.

Evaluation

- Harold's friend always goes along with Harold's crazy ideas. What might have happened in the story if Harold's friend had not always supported his ideas? How would this change the storyline and the themes in the book?

- Harold is a science whiz but lacks skills in the social arena. What are some other things that Harold is good at, and what things could he improve upon? Evaluate which of Harold's actions you think are right and which ones are mistakes. In your opinion, what skills are the most important ones to have in middle school, and why?

- Imagine that your guidance counselor has asked you to write a letter to Harold to help him have more friends. Evaluate Harold's actions in the book, and then write him a letter explaining what you think he should do to make more friends, as well as what you think are some important skills and behaviors for someone to have in middle school.

The Schernoff Discoveries
by Gary Paulsen

Activity: In-Depth Discussion

Group students into pairs, and ask each group to complete the questions below. Then, have the groups return to the whole group and share their responses to the questions. An in-depth discussion of this kind will allow the students to better understand how themes in a book can relate to different contexts.

Identify two central themes or ideas in the book.

1. _____

_____

2. _____

_____

Find and copy a quote from the text that supports each theme that you identified. If you can find a quote that supports both themes, you do not need to find a second one.

1. _____

_____

2. _____

_____

Evaluate why these themes are important to everyday life.

_____

_____

_____

How do these themes relate to:

Life in society, in which we have to get along with others (social context)?

_____

_____

Life in other times and places (historical context)?

_____

_____

Your own, personal, everyday life (personal context)?

_____

_____

Chapter 6
The Importance of Communication

> *Competence in interpersonal relationships is probably the single most important factor in determining whether or not gifted children will be successful, caring, contributing members of society.*
>
> -James T. Webb

🖉 Chapter Highlights

➤ Communication tips for parents and teachers

➤ Information on methods of communication, including using technology, newsletters, meetings, surveys, and conferences

➤ Effectives ways for teachers to conduct meetings and conferences with parents and with students

🖉 Research Connections

➤ J. Bruzzese (2009), *A Parent's Guide to the Middle School Years*

➤ B. J. Gilman (2008), *Academic Advocacy for Gifted Children: A Parent's Complete Guide*

➤ K. B. Rogers (2002), *Re-Forming Gifted Education: How Parents and Teachers Can Match the Program to the Child*

➤ D. Ruf (2005), *5 Levels of Gifted: School Issues and Educational Options*

➤ J. F. Smutny (2000), *Stand Up for Your Gifted Child: How to Make the Most of Kids' Strengths at School and at Home*

➤ C. A. Strip (2000), *Helping Gifted Children Soar*

Teachers, parents, administrators, counselors, and students all play an important part in the academic, social, and emotional issues that exist in middle schools today. While these individuals all agree that good communication is essential when working with gifted students, everyday pressures and time constraints sometimes interfere. Teachers, who must work hard to address a wide range of student abilities in their heterogeneously grouped classrooms, have little time left for communicating with parents. Parents, busy with their jobs and maintaining a household, find it hard to schedule time to talk with teachers.

This chapter contains information about communication in general, and between teachers and parents in particular. It is far easier to resolve issues relating to a student's reading achievement when parents and teachers can talk effectively with one another. In addition, adults who communicate to solve problems are modeling important skills, which will help their teens learn to successfully communicate as well. Several ideas to help parents and teachers communicate effectively follow.

Parents Communicating with Teachers

Avoid the "Pushy Parent" Label

Parents of gifted students want reading instruction and school experiences that promote academic, social, and emotional growth in their children. Because their children need academic challenge that is beyond the normal middle school curriculum, many parents of gifted teens find that they must advocate for their children. Approaching teachers in the wrong way, however, often has a negative effect and can ruin what the parents are trying to accomplish. If parents come on too strong, voicing their opinions or stating their questions in ways that come across as "pushy," teachers can feel threatened, become defensive, and resist anything that the parent has to say. Thus, it is important for parents to learn positive ways to communicate with teachers.

There are several ways for parents to become effective advocates for their children. One of the most important things to remember is that it is far more beneficial for parents to become partners with their children's teachers rather than adversaries of them. Cooperation between school and home can be very powerful in contributing to students' current and future successes (Gilman, 2008). Part of this process involves parents following the chain of command when communicating with the school. This means that their first contact is with the child's teacher. Parents should give the teacher a chance to rectify the situation before going to a higher authority. In the case of gifted middle schoolers, talking to a teacher first might mean talking with just the homeroom teacher or a teacher who teaches a particular subject, or in some cases, it could mean requesting a meeting with the entire team of teachers who instruct the student.

If parents are concerned with a lack of challenge in their child's reading program, they should begin by voicing this concern to the child's English teacher. This allows the parent to hear the teacher's point of view, and it shows respect for the teacher. In some cases, especially near the beginning of the year, the teacher may simply be unaware that the child is unhappy. Many gifted teens don't want to bring attention to themselves by displaying signs that they are frustrated or bored—this is, after all, the time period during which they most want to fit in. When parents discuss their child's lack of challenge with the teacher, it gives the teacher information that she may not have had that will allow her to make modifications to the reading content. If, after several conversations with the teacher, the situation does not improve, then it is appropriate for the parents to make an appointment with the principal. Parents should not complain to a school board member unless they have first tried to resolve the problem at the local school level. When parents go behind the teacher or the principal to a school board member, they are undermining both the principal and the teacher by not giving them a chance to correct the problem first.

If parents are hesitant to talk with their child's teacher, they might first talk with the school counselor to get advice on an appropriate way to handle the concern. Sometimes parents can even encourage their children to talk to the teacher directly about their complaint. Gifted children benefit from learning communication and negotiation skills; these are skills that they will use throughout their lives. The parent and child could role-play the conversation at home first, with the parent acting as the teacher. It may be that the teacher would allow the student to do a different assignment that would meet the curricular goals of the unit of study but would offer the student more appropriate challenge. Educators are nearly always open to some modification of the curriculum if it would better meet individual student needs.

Homework for Parents

As students leave elementary school to go on to the busy middle school environment, they may experience an overload of emotions and expectations. Middle school relationships between kids jump up to a whole new level of ambiguity, and both adolescents and parents often become frustrated by these intense new peer relationships (Bruzzese, 2009). This, combined with the adjustment that students must make to break away from the easy environment of elementary school and move to a schedule of different subject area teachers, creates a great deal of stress, which increases the need for effective communication.

Gifted children need to have a voice in decisions about their education (Smutny, 2000). If parents don't know what is taking place in their child's classes, the first place to start is to ask the child. Too often, parents make judgments based on what they see coming home, but this is not necessarily an accurate way to assess what a child is doing in school. Thus, parents must interact with their child in ways that will allow the child to feel comfortable opening up to them. Good communication will build a relationship of trust that will eventually lead to a student's willingness to share information about what happens during his or her time at school.

Parents, if your child needs some sort of intervention at school to make assignments more interesting, talk to him or her about actions you'd like to take. Discuss options. Ask: *What would make school more interesting? If you could change anything in school, what would you change? When do you feel most excited about classes? When do you tune out?* Your child's responses to these types of questions will give you important information about what is happening in the curriculum and where your child may need greater challenge.

With this information as a starting point, parents will need to do some more homework in order to be effective advocates for their gifted children (Smutny, 2000):

> ➤ Collect background information about policies and practices of other local school districts. This will help you determine if your child's school is doing what is it

supposed to be doing when dealing with gifted readers. Parents can contact their State Department of Education to gather information about what schools are required to do for gifted students. Some states have a legal mandate for schools to provide appropriate education for gifted and talented children. The information will help you make decisions about future actions.

➤ Learn all you can about programming for gifted students and what gifted students need. As a parent of a gifted reader, it helps to know if the gifted program in your child's school will differentiate reading instruction within classrooms or whether it requires gifted students be pulled out of their regular classrooms for reading instruction.

➤ Set up a time to meet with school officials, and have a written plan for what you are requesting before the meeting takes place. Request that child's current teacher and the person in charge of gifted curriculum and/or the school psychologist be present at the meeting.

➤ When talking with teachers, express concerns and ideas in a diplomatic way, but be firm. Thank teachers for taking time to meet and talk about progress. Get right to the point without talking about other issues or sharing information about other teachers. Once the conversation begins, listen carefully so that teachers do not perceive the meeting as one-sided.

➤ Finally, try to work together to create solutions. Plan a follow-up meeting to check progress.

As a parent, you play a critical role in the education of your gifted children. You have known your child for her entire life; teachers know your child for only one year. You will probably be more influential in the way your child matures and develops than any teacher could be. It is important to remain a positive advocate when addressing her needs. Staying positive also models persistence and problem solving for your child.

Parents who want more information about advocating for their children (and teachers who want to learn more about classroom options for gifted students) can find specific suggestions from a number of resource books written for parents. In *Helping Gifted Children Soar* (2000), Carol Strip strongly supports parents and teachers communicating and working together for the benefit of gifted children. She suggests that parents and teachers become a team working to meet the child's needs. Parents should share information with the teacher about what the child is like at home, and teachers in turn should tell parents what the child is like at school. Both parents and teachers may be unaware of how the child behaves in the other setting, and these revelations can lead to insights and solutions that might not otherwise be evident.

Another valuable resource is a book titled *Re-Forming Gifted Education: How Parents and Teachers Can Match the Program to the Child* (Rogers, 2002). In this book, Karen Rogers, a leading researcher in the field of gifted education, describes a variety of flexible educational options for gifted programming that are fairly easy for schools to implement, including various types of acceleration, enrichment, and grouping, as well as how to develop an education plan for your child and then present it to the school. This education plan addresses both the academic and the social and emotional needs of the gifted child.

Still another helpful resource is *Academic Advocacy for Gifted Children* (Gilman, 2008), a book packed full of good information on how to effectively advocate for gifted children in middle and high school. In it, the author also shares her personal story of how she took advocacy a step further, as she, along with other parents in her community, lobbied for and actually created a middle school specifically designed to meet the needs of gifted adolescents.

If you think your child may be highly or exceptionally gifted, look for the book *5 Levels of Gifted* (Ruf, 2005), which describes children at various levels of giftedness by grouping them by their developmental milestones. This book is fascinating reading for teachers as well. It reminds them that they might have an exceptionally or profoundly gifted child in their classroom, and it tells them how to recognize such a child. Ruf also describes the type of education that children at each level of giftedness need.

In addition to books as resources, there is a great deal of helpful information on the Internet. Helpful websites for both parents and teachers include:

- ➤ www.hoagiesgifted.org
- ➤ www.nagc.org
- ➤ www.sengifted.org
- ➤ www.GreatPotentialPress.com
- ➤ www.FreeSpiritPublishing.com
- ➤ www.PrufrockPress.com.

A Checklist for Parents

Parents: *The checklist below contains valuable points that will promote and enhance open communication with your middle school gifted child's classroom teachers. It will also help you organize your thoughts and ideas when communicating with teachers about specific concerns throughout the school year.*

- ❏ I have received information about the English program at my child's school, and I understand ways in which the teacher differentiates reading instruction for my child.

- ❏ I feel comfortable talking with my child about school-related issues.

- ❏ I have started to collect resources such as books, journals, and lists of websites that will help me better understand my gifted adolescent student. These resources include those regarding educational options for gifted students, and they provide me with ways to effectively communicate with staff members at the middle school.

- ❏ I have introduced myself to my child's teachers at the middle school and expressed my desire to have regular communication regarding the gifted program, progress made by my child, and any concerns that the teacher may have during the school year. I have provided a means for teachers to reach me so they may share important information.

- ❏ I understand that I can request meetings with my child's team of teachers in order to gather information about the curriculum in his or her English class.

- ❏ I understand that parent-teacher communication is essential, but it is sometimes difficult to schedule a meeting at the middle school level because interdisciplinary teams of teachers maintain different teaching schedules.

- ❏ I understand that gifted students may sometimes exhibit behaviors that can that can lead to potential problems in the classroom. This is why communication with staff members is critical in middle school.

- ❏ I understand that no two gifted children are alike and that I should not compare my son or daughter with other gifted students.

- ❏ I realize that it is important to monitor my child's completion of homework or other classroom assignments.

- ❏ I realize that some situations do not have a clear answer or solution and that it is important for me to work with the team of teachers with a fair and open mind. With this understanding, I also realize that it is important to identify who "owns" the problem so that I'll know when it is appropriate to get involved and when I need to let my child handle the problem on his or her own.

- ❏ If I have questions or become frustrated, I should first look, listen, and examine. I can *look* at ways my child is acting and responding to questions about school. I can *listen* when my child needs to talk about his or her reading experiences. I can *examine* by checking with teachers and other staff to see if my child is representing the situation accurately, and if necessary, I can talk to my child about behaviors that are needed for success in school.

Teachers Communicating with Parents

Communication with parents is one of the most important components of effective gifted programs. If teachers and administrators want students to achieve success, they must work together to create ways for two-way sharing with parents.

Practice Being Proactive and Not Reactive

When their children reach middle school, parents often find that they are anxious for their young teens to adapt to the new school environment. Because these adolescent children are beginning a period of growth and development, as well as identity formation during which they are trying to separate from their parents and become independent from them, they often do not communicate well with their parents during this time. Consequently, parents often find themselves frustrated by the many unknowns that exist in their child's middle school (Bruzzese, 2009).

To help relieve some of this stress and frustration during these times of uncertainty, it is helpful if teachers develop systems for communicating directly with parents. Even if teachers are unaware of specific concerns that parents may have, it is reasonable to expect that many parents will naturally exhibit some of these feelings, and a teacher stance of being *proactive* instead of *reactive* in the communication process is likely to be much welcomed by parents.

Using Technology to Communicate

While face-to-face meetings are probably the best and most appropriate way to talk with parents, they aren't always possible due to both parent and teacher schedules. When time constraints are an issue, keeping parents informed via email is an option. Teachers can request email addresses from parents at the beginning of the school year (promising not to share them with others without permission). Be sure to ask parents for permission to send messages to them, since some people are not allowed to receive personal email at work, and others prefer phone calls as a way of sharing information about their child. Starting "on the same page" helps when creating effective communication strategies.

Some parents (and also students) have requested that teachers create websites or blogs as a method for communication. Teachers can ask which method parents prefer. In either case, modern technology makes more frequent communication with parents easy and effective.

Monthly Newsletters

Another method for teachers to communicate with parents is the use of a monthly newsletter. Most parents appreciate receiving a newsletter each month that explains what is taking place in English and reading instruction in their child's school, including goals and progress for the advanced readers. It is a good idea for teachers to print out the newsletters on colored paper and use the same color every month. As a parent of a 15-year-old gifted son, I endorse this practice. Once I realized that a bright green newsletter was coming home the last Friday of each month, it was easy to find this document in the mess of papers in my son's bookbag. When teachers establish a consistent pattern of communication, parents will learn to watch for and be aware of it. As many parents can tell you, student backpacks are frequently full of random papers and foreign objects. Distinguishing a love letter from the girl who sits behind your son in English class from a newsletter outlining the progress of the gifted readers in the class will be easier if the teacher uses the same format each time.

A sample newsletter is included on the following page.

Informational Meetings with Parents of Gifted Students

Instead of holding individual meetings with parents of each gifted student, teachers may find it helpful to hold one large group meeting, perhaps at the fall Open House, to describe the reading program to parents of middle school gifted readers. At this meeting, the teacher can discuss the books she plans to study throughout the year, the methods of differentiating instruction that she will use so that gifted readers are challenged, and the ways she plans to communicate and assess progress throughout the year. When parents begin the year with an understanding of the program for their gifted and advanced readers, it paves the way for them to support the teacher from the start, as well as for real student learning to take place in the months that follow.

Surveys

Communication between teachers and parents involves teachers not only providing information to parents, but also receiving information from parents. One way for teachers to get information from parents is to simply ask for it in the form of surveys and inventories that will allow them learn more about their gifted readers. When creating a survey to send to parents, teachers should not only ask for input regarding students' interests and abilities in reading, but they should also explain the purpose of the survey—to learn about student interests in order to create appropriate assignments and instruction. A sample Reading Interest Survey appears on page 166.

Sample Teacher Newsletter

The Gifted Digest from Room 5

CURRENT EVENTS

Exciting things continue to happen in our English class. The students have read different novels that were selected based on individual ability levels. As they read their books, they participated in open discussions that allowed for critical inquiry and self-reflection. They also explored advanced vocabulary and evaluated decisions and actions portrayed by main characters. After reading, students demonstrated understanding by completing projects that extended their literature experiences. Several students produced TV broadcasts that included "reporters" interviewing "characters" from the books. Other students created posters that displayed their comprehension of main themes and literary elements. We were pleased with the high quality of their projects.

RECOMMENDED READING

○ Rimm, S. B. (2008). *How to parent so children will learn*. Scottsdale, AZ: Great Potential Press.

○ Tomlinson, C. A., & Eidson, C. C. (2003). *Differentiation in practice: A resource guide for differentiating curriculum, grades 5-9*. Alexandria, VA: Association for Supervision and Curriculum Development.

○ Webb, J. T., Gore, J. L., Amend, E. R., & DeVries, A. R. (2007). *A parent's guide to gifted children*. Scottsdale, AZ: Great Potential Press.

○ Willis, J. A. (2009). *Inspiring middle school minds: Gifted, creative, and challenging*. Scottsdale, AZ: Great Potential Press.

WHAT'S COMING UP?

Mark your calendars for **Community Sharing Day**. This event will take place on October 10th at 1:00 pm. Parents and community members are invited to come and interact with students as they explain their book projects. We'll serve light refreshments. This is a great way to learn more about our class and the curriculum we are implementing. We hope to see everyone on the 10th!

After Community Sharing Day, each student will choose a new book to read in English class. We encourage the students to choose a book that is based on their individual interests. After reading, the students will learn about Socratic seminars. They will discover ways to question their own thinking processes while evaluating their reading progress. Final projects will promote opportunities to synthesize and analyze information they found in their books.

PARENT RESOURCE CORNER

The following suggestions will help you reinforce and extend your child's learning at home:

✏ Ask to see homework assignments on a regular basis, and generate dialog with your adolescent student about his or her work in school.

✏ Read books and other articles that relate to gifted education.

✏ Talk with your child about his or her interests throughout the school year.

Reading Interest Survey

Date: _____

Dear Parents or Guardians:

In an effort to provide my students with opportunities to read books that are not only challenging, but that also allow for the development of critical thinking, I am asking for your input. Please take the time to complete this survey. It will help me reach my goal of increasing reading performances among students in my class and will help you focus on the needs of your child. If you feel uncomfortable with any of the questions below, you can leave the space blank, or you may call me at school. I will return your call in a timely manner. I believe that together we can make a difference.

1. How often does your child participate in leisure reading at home? What sorts of things does your child like to read?

   _____

   _____

2. Do you find it a challenge to motivate your child to read? Please explain.

   _____

   _____

   _____

3. What is your opinion of your child's previous experiences in English? Have your child's experiences with reading and language arts been positive? If not, what would have made these experiences better?

   _____

   _____

   _____

4. When and how did you first realize your child was advanced in reading?

   _____

   _____

5. If given a choice, would your child choose to read fiction or nonfiction?

   _____

   _____

6. Are there certain areas of language arts that you would like your child to improve in this school year? Please explain.

   _____

   _____

Teachers Communicating with Students

Student-Teacher Conferences

Adolescents are generally ruled by emotion. The parts of their brains that process reason aren't fully developed yet, and research suggests that the more gifted the student, the slower this development occurs (Willis, 2009). Therefore, when teachers communicate with their students—especially their gifted ones—they must do so in ways that ensure that the students fully understand how they are doing and what is expected of them in the future.

One method that is effective for middle schoolers is the student-teacher conference. Chapter 7 contains more information about this method as it relates to assessment. However, holding a conference to talk with a student does not always mean just talking about grades or performances. Conferences can be set up on a regular basis so that students know they will have opportunities to speak with the teacher in a one-to-one format. These conferences can cover a wide range of topics or concerns, so it is wise to have a focus and a goal established before conducting the conference.

To ensure a successful student-teacher conference, teachers should observe the following points:

➤ Try to make the student feel comfortable. If you need to speak with the student about something that is private, make sure there is no one else within earshot.

➤ If you feel that parents need to be involved, talk with the student first and let the student know that you will be inviting his parents. This shows respect for the student and allows him to begin accepting responsibility for his own learning and progress.

➤ Make sure that everything is documented during these meetings, even for those conferences that are just "counseling" or "coaching" sessions or follow-up meetings. This is important to protect both teachers and students. Keep this documentation secured so that the student's privacy is protected.

The following pages include two sample forms for teachers wishing to hold conferences with students as a means of improving communication. The first is a pre-conference form. The teacher should give the students this form prior to the student-teacher conference, allowing them ample time to think about their answers before filling it out. The teacher can then collect and review the forms before each individual conference. The forms provide the teacher with valuable information about how the student feels and what his or her expectations and needs are so that the meeting can include discussion of specific goals and objectives for the student.

The second form is a follow-up form to fill out after the student-teacher conference takes place. This form should be filled out by both the student and the teacher, as it includes places to write specific goals for improvement by both parties for the rest of the school year. Teachers can refer back to this form in future conferences to see if those goals are being met.

Pre-Conference Form for Students

Name:_____ Date:_____

Teacher:_____ Class:_____

1. The most important thing that I am trying to do well this year is:
_____
_____

2. This is important to me because:
_____
_____

3. Other things that I am proud of this year are:
_____
_____

4. I am working as hard as I can to achieve and to learn the most that I can. (*If this is true, justify or explain your answer. If it is not, what can you improve?*)
_____
_____

5. If I could do one thing over this school year, I would:
_____
_____

6. In my classes next year, I want to:
_____
_____

7. Two things that I need to work harder at are:
   1._____
   2._____

8. My goal(s) for the rest of the school year is/are:
_____
_____

Student Signature:_____ Date:_____

Student-Teacher Conference Follow-Up Form

Name:_____ Date:_____

Teacher:_____ Class:_____

Directions: *During our student-teacher conference on _____(date), we identified some areas in which you wanted to improve. We also discussed areas in which I could improve in order to meet your needs. Please complete this agreement by summarizing our discussion and the decisions that we made during our conference.*

Conference notes:

_____

_____

_____

_____

Ways the student can improve:

_____

_____

_____

_____

Ways the teacher can improve:

_____

_____

_____

_____

Together, we will make this year a successful year. We need to communicate with each other so that changes may be made if needed.

Student Signature:_____

Teacher Signature:_____

Suggestion Box

Another way for teachers to encourage communication with their students is to set up a suggestion box. Sometimes students are hesitant to speak up in class, and this can be especially true of gifted students. A suggestion box is one way to let everyone, even those students who are shy, feel comfortable about letting their voice be heard. Students can ask questions about assignments or state concerns about issues by writing notes or questions on index cards and placing them in the box. One of the primary benefits of this method is that students can choose to remain anonymous. They can sign their name on their card if they want, but they do not have to. The teacher can then read the cards after class and respond appropriately, without revealing the identity of the student who wrote the question or suggestion.

✎ Key Points

1. Students in middle school are often poor at communicating with adults for a variety of reasons. Thus, parents and teachers must learn to effectively communicate with one another.

2. Teachers, parents, administrators, counselors, and students all play an important role in the communication process.

3. Parents should approach educators with respect and an open mind.

4. Teachers should be proactive instead of reactive when communicating with parents.

5. Newsletters, meetings, surveys, conferences, and the Internet are all effective methods for communicating among teachers, parents, and students.

6. When parents are well informed, they are more supportive of teacher efforts.

Chapter 7

Assessment of Gifted Readers in Middle School

> *Since assessment drives curriculum for many middle school teachers, the types of assessment they use in the classroom are very important.*
>
> ~Amy Horn

✎ Chapter Highlights

➤ The role of assessment in the curriculum framework

➤ Methods for evaluating or assessing gifted readers in middle school

➤ How to create opportunities for students to reflect on their own progress and achievement

✎ Research Connections

➤ P. A. Facione & N. C. Facione (1994), *The Holistic Critical Thinking Scoring Rubric: A Tool for Developing and Evaluating Critical Thinking*

➤ National Middle School Association (2010), *This We Believe: Successful Schools for Young Adolescents*

➤ J. VanTassel-Baska (2002), *Planning Effective Curriculum Experiences for Gifted Learners*

Assessment Drives Curriculum

Imagine this scenario. A group of teachers sits anxiously in the library waiting for the principal to begin a faculty meeting with a summary of scores from standardized tests. Some talk about their busy day while others reflect upon the last six months of school.

Thoughts like these are in their heads: *Did we focus our attention on the right benchmarks? I hope the scores indicate achievement for my students. If the scores show a decrease in reading achievement, then our entire English program will change.*

As they hear the door close and see the principal walk into the library with a binder that contains test scores for the all the students in the school, the teachers are brought back to reality. Everyone in the room takes a deep breath as they anticipate a heated discussion about changes in their curriculum.

Teachers around the country feel similar emotions as they wait to see how their students have scored on standardized tests. They know that their curriculum will likely change due to the results of these formal tests, because test results typically lead to the creation of new strategies to help increase student achievement. Though settings differ, teacher responses and reactions remain the same; teachers know that what is taught in classrooms correlates with scores that come from both formal and informal assessments.

Most educators agree that assessment must guide curriculum development. However, educators must also acknowledge that the decision to change curriculum should reflect several indicators of achievement and should not be based on a one-time evaluation. It is vital that teachers understand that assessment is an ongoing process that provides glimpses of student progress at different points in time. As teachers strive to meet the needs of their students, they must remember the following:

➤ Assessment drives curriculum.
➤ Assessment must be ongoing.
➤ Assessment must be implemented using multiple measures in order to reach all students.

There are many assessment strategies that teachers can use to facilitate the evaluation process. Joyce VanTassel-Baska (2002), a leading researcher in gifted education, supports using multiple measures and approaches for assessing gifted learners in classrooms. She states that the purpose of the assessment process is really multi-dimensional because it provides insights into student progress in a curriculum and identifies future needs for all learners.

Assessment Strategies

The National Middle School Association supports heterogeneous groupings of students in the middle school setting (National Middle School Association, 2010). Yet middle school teachers continue to voice concerns about the difficulties they encounter as they strive to meet the needs of heterogeneous classrooms, in which reading levels can vary as much as five or six grades. Trying to create lessons for such diverse ability levels places incredible demands on teachers.

Because teachers must develop lessons that are differentiated based on the needs of their students, they quickly realize that they also need alternate assessment techniques to measure progress made by individual students. If methods for delivering instruction are different in classrooms with gifted learners, then assessment needs to be different as well. For this reason, it is important for teachers of gifted students to become familiar with a variety of assessment methods to use in various situations. Historically, quizzes and tests were the tools teachers used to gauge student progress, but a test that is too easy for a bright student does not measure that student's progress.

The following principles will assist teachers in developing alternate assessment strategies for gifted learners (Van Tassel-Baska, 2002):

➤ Assessment should incorporate both long-term and short-term measures. This approach supports the theory that a combination of frequent quizzes and less-frequent tests is a better way to measure student learning than the use of just one or the other.

➤ Teachers should use multiple and varied types of measures. This includes portfolios of students' work, product evaluation, and observational checklists.

In middle school, assessment has several different purposes and comes in many different forms. Educators can use a variety of assessment strategies to help them become better, more effective teachers and to help students become more accomplished learners. There are three approaches to assessment that can be used interchangeably to support student achievement, as well as gather evidence of what a student knows, understands, and is able to do. These areas include the following:

➤ *Assessment for Learning* – Collecting and evaluating information in order to plan and prepare future assignments

➤ *Assessment as Learning* – Collecting and evaluating information to help students become active participants in their own learning

➤ *Assessment of Learning* – Collecting and evaluating information to determine strengths and weaknesses after units have been completed or content has been introduced

The following chart identifies several student assessment methods.

Overview of Assessment Methods

Assessment *for* Learning	Assessment *as* Learning	Assessment *of* Learning
Pre-tests	Self-assessment	Formal tests
Observations	Peer assessment	Standardized tests
Classroom questions and/or discussion	Student conferences	Tests used with adopted textbooks
	Portfolios	
	Rubrics	

When most people think of assessment, they really only think of the third part of this assessment triad—assessment *of* learning. The rest of this chapter describes and defines each of the first two areas of assessment further. With the examples and strategies that follow, teachers of gifted readers will understand how assessment plays an important role in student achievement.

Assessment *for* Learning

Assessment for learning is used when teachers measure students' understanding in order to plan or create lessons. When students are heterogeneously grouped, teachers know that they are not all working at the same ability or achievement levels. It becomes important to know what material individual students have already mastered and how to take them further in their learning. Assessing students in order to obtain information as to where they are in relation to other students or where they are when looking at personal achievement will help teachers provide more appropriate learning experiences for them.

Understanding policies set forth by schools and school districts will aid educators as they develop tools to help evaluate students' understanding of particular benchmarks. A fair practice is to allow students who demonstrate mastery in specific areas to move forward by participating in curriculum compacting opportunities or learning contracts so that they can progress to learning new material.

A pre-test is a good way to discover how much each student knows about a topic or unit before the teacher begins teaching the unit. Pre-tests not only provide information about what students already know, they also lead to better student-teacher relationships. When gifted students realize that they will have opportunities to demonstrate their knowledge, they feel as if their teachers truly believe in their abilities and efforts. The message from the teacher is: *I believe that your time is valuable. Some of you may already have mastered this concept. Therefore, I am giving you a chance to show me what you already know so that I can give you alternate assignments when appropriate.* An atmosphere of mutual respect begins to develop when teachers offer students the opportunity to demonstrate their understanding. Teachers can then use the information they gain from the pre-tests to tailor curriculum and create assignments that are better suited to individual students.

Mr. Jensen, a middle school English teacher, had planned for the students in his class to read The Call of the Wild *by Jack London. When Kris shared that she had already read the book, she and Mr. Jensen talked quietly about it while the other students were immersed in their reading. This discussion served as an informal pre-test and demonstrated to Mr. Jensen that Kris understood the themes in the book and had enjoyed reading it. Mr. Jensen then asked Kris what sort of book she would like to read instead while the rest of the class read and discussed* The Call of the Wild. *Kris said that she was interested in learning about American Indians—their history and lifestyle in the West. Mr. Jensen promised to find a book for Kris to read that would incorporate this interest. The book that Kris chose from several suggested by the school librarian was* Sitting Bull and His World *by Albert Martin. Mr. Jensen made up an individual learning contract for the work that Kris would do. In it, Kris agreed to share with the rest of the class what she learned about Sitting Bull and the disappearance of the great herds of buffalo. Mr. Jensen agreed to read the book as well so that he could later discuss the various themes with Kris in a one-to-one conference. Kris understood that she would participate in class discussions of* The Call of the Wild, *but she would not be required to complete the assignments or quizzes related to that book.*

Teachers looking for tools to assess gifted readers in middle school should also observe students and document student behaviors on checklists or in anecdotal records. Observing and taking brief notes on a student's ability, motivation, and desire will help teachers gain a better understanding of where the student is operating in terms of reading comprehension and understanding of literary elements. Recording students' responses to questions that have been posed to generate higher levels of thought will also help middle school teachers assess gifted readers' abilities to effectively respond to critical reading opportunities.

Assessment as Learning

There are many assessment strategies and techniques that can be used in classrooms with gifted readers that provide evaluative information as learning occurs. This area of assessment includes students in the daily task of keeping track of their own learning as they become active participants in the assessment process. Strategies include self-assessment, peer assessment, portfolio assessment, student conferences, and rubrics.

Self-Assessment

One way to engage gifted students in their learning is through self-assessment. When students evaluate their own work, they take ownership of their successes and their mistakes. Sometimes teachers need to guide students, especially those who are new to self-assessment, to show them where their work is truly good and where it needs some improvement. Gifted students can be hard on themselves and can set up rigorous standards to maintain, and this is particularly true for those adolescents who have perfectionistic tendencies. These students may find fault with nearly everything they do for their classes. Conversely, some gifted students believe that, having achieved top scores without effort in elementary school, they don't have to put much effort into their work in middle school either. Teachers need to gently coach students like these to push themselves to reach not just acceptable work, but work that is a true testament of that which they are capable.

One way for teachers to help students learn how to measure their work in as objective a manner as possible is to give them various self-assessment forms to fill out. The teacher can look over these forms and then compare the student's notes with the teacher's own appraisal of how the student did on a particular assignment or project. Talking with the student about how their two views compare can teach students to measure their success with appropriate standards.

The major benefit of self-assessment forms is that they teach students to evaluate their own work, which will enable them to adjust their learning methods to create more successes for themselves in the future. In this way, self-assessment drives students to progress through continual self-examination and readjustment.

Sample self-assessment forms are included in this chapter for students to use to assess their portfolios and student conferences.

Peer Assessment

Students can learn not only how to assess themselves, but also how to assess each other. Teachers can have students swap work with one another to offer a peer review of the quality of each student's work. The key to successful peer assessment, however, is for teachers to make sure that those students who are trading work for peer appraisal are true peers—not just because they are the same age or because they happen to have been placed in the same class, but because they are academic and intellectual equals (or are at least close). It is extremely frustrating for gifted students to have their work "corrected" erroneously by students who are not as advanced in their ability or comprehension. It is also hard for students who are not gifted to have their work "torn to shreds" by students who are far more advanced in their intellectual capabilities. Intellectual peers can give much more thoughtful and constructive feedback than those students who are unevenly matched. When students are paired with others of similar ability, peer assessment can be a helpful tool that offers them a different perspective than that which the teacher can give.

Teachers should coach students on how to give one another constructive feedback. A student who just tells another that he liked what she wrote or who gives only positive feedback because the two are friends may be nice, but he is not being very helpful. Teachers should require that these evaluations include specific comments about what the student thought was good and why, as well as any suggestions for what could make the work better.

Student Conferences

As previously noted, the middle school years not only provide challenges for teachers, but for students as well. The elementary years are over, which means the amount of one-on-one time with a teacher is now limited. Whereas elementary teachers work with the same group of students throughout the entire year, most middle school teachers typically deal with 100 to 150 students per day as the students move from one class to the next. Having such a large number of students creates frustration and stress for teachers as they attempt to meet the individual academic and instructional needs of all of these children. The large number of students is also an issue when searching for effective ways to communicate and assess this population.

It is crucial for teachers who work with students at the middle school level to find ways to communicate individually with students. Not only will this help facilitate more appropriate assessment opportunities, it also provides time for teachers and students to express their thoughts about individual student progress.

Organizing conferences in which students, parents, and teachers all play an important role helps promote communication and gives relevance to classwork. These joint conferences not only help students take ownership of their learning, they also give students an opportunity to practice important communication skills that they will need throughout their lives—in high school, college, and eventually in the world of work. Conferences can become an integral part of student learning, as well as a regular feature within the classroom.

Teachers who wish to involve parents and students in assessment routines can begin scheduling conferences in which students and parents are both important participants. This type of conference is quite different from the traditional conference in which the teacher is the chief communicator and the parents hear how their child is doing in class. In this new type of student-parent-teacher conference, the student becomes the leader of the conversation. If appropriate, the student plans the conference, decides the content of the conference, and chooses which work samples to share during the conference. The teacher serves as a guide while the student showcases his work and discusses his efforts for his parents. It's a wonderful way for a maturing student to take pride in and responsibility for his schoolwork. However, it is important that the teacher be able to bring up issues about areas that need improvement or other concerns that she may have. In such situations, the teacher should discuss the matter with the student before the meeting so there are no surprises on the day of the conference.

This type of assessment method promotes open communication among all parties involved in a child's education; thus, many teachers use it as a means of talking with parents. Having students analyze and make judgments regarding their own work prior to the conference also makes this strategy effective for assessment purposes.

Teachers can help gifted students in middle school prepare for this kind of self-assessment by asking them to reflect on certain areas. This might include things they learned that were important, areas in which they need to improve, their reasons and evidence for believing this way, and goals for the next quarter or term. Once this reflection process takes place, teachers should encourage students to gather work samples to be presented on the day of the conference. Students usually feel comfortable discussing their work samples with their parents during the conference because they helped make these selections based on their own personal reflections and analyses.

If students are not comfortable taking the lead when discussing their progress and achievement during conferences that include their parents, the teacher can certainly take on this role. In this case, the student, the parents, and the teacher each take turns communicating their opinions, questions, concerns, and the student's progress. During this type of assessment, it is recommended that the teacher take notes to document the meeting so that everyone leaves with the same information and understanding of what should take place in the future. This will also help protect the teacher if further questions arise or if administrators have questions about the methods used for assessing students.

The following page contains a form for teachers to give to students so that they can summarize the conference and clarify their goals for the rest of the school year. In addition, it asks students to note areas in which they have made improvements, allowing them to focus on the positive aspects of learning and doing well in school.

Student Conference Self-Assessment Form

Name:_____ Date:_____

Those in attendance:

_____   _____

_____   _____

_____   _____

I have made improvement in the following areas:

_____

_____

_____

_____

_____

My goals for the next quarter or term:

_____

_____

_____

_____

_____

How I plan to achieve my goals:

_____

_____

_____

_____

_____

_____

Sample Letter to Parents

Date:

Dear Parents,

I am pleased to tell you about a new method I am implementing to assess students in my classroom using conferences. I believe it is important for students to be involved in their learning, and I also feel that it is extremely beneficial for them to understand what is being evaluated, as well as the role they play in their own assessment.

What makes this different from other conferences is the fact that your child will be the chief communicator while I will serve as a guide to help him or her express him- or herself. Your child will soon give you an invitation with a date and time for the conference.

During the conference, you will have the opportunity to view your child's work samples, as well as discuss your child's goals and future plans. You will have an opportunity to ask questions about curriculum and instruction that takes place on a daily basis. I believe this method of assessment and communication helps students in several ways: they become more engaged in their own learning, and they begin to take more responsibility for their work and their actions.

If you have concerns that you wish to discuss privately, please call me or send me an email. I am always available to answer questions that you might have pertaining to your child's progress and achievement. I look forward to meeting with you and your child as we look at current progress and communicate future goals.

Sincerely,

Mrs. Armstrong
Seventh-Grade English Teacher

Portfolio Assessment

A portfolio is a collection of work samples that communicates a student's interests and gives evidence of the student's performance. It serves as a record-keeping tool that highlights for others what the student has learned, accomplished, and/or produced. Teachers should establish specific guidelines for the contents of portfolios, as well as a list of criteria for evaluation of the work, including evidence that students were able to reflect upon their own learning and experiences. Teachers and students should work together throughout the year to choose work samples to be included in the portfolio.

Portfolios can contain samples of student written work, for example, which shows progress in writing skills from one semester to the next. They can also contain tests and quizzes, as well as graphic organizers or illustrations that the student may have created for certain assignments. If a student completes a hands-on project such as a diorama, a photograph of the project can be included in the portfolio as evidence of the achievement. An advantage of portfolios is that they provide concrete evidence of individual student performance over an extended period of time and thus show student growth.

Martin Kimeldore (1994) suggests several different ways to set up and organize a portfolio so that it fits students' needs. Work samples for portfolios may be selected and organized in a variety of ways:

- ➤ In chronological order of work samples completed
- ➤ By level of complexity
- ➤ By skills, talents, or areas of knowledge
- ➤ By a particular theme
- ➤ By using a combination of the above options
- ➤ According to other teacher requirements

One seventh-grade English teacher who uses portfolios has students include in them: (1) one piece of their writing each month to show progress, (2) a test or other product from each unit studied, (3) a grammar exercise in which the student made corrections to a deliberately poor piece of writing, (4) a creative project, (5) a research project about a career that interests them, and (6) three poems the student liked, with notes from the student in the margins. Students can select items from their portfolio to show their parents at the student-parent-teacher conference to demonstrate their progress in English.

Student Portfolio Self-Assessment Form

Name:_____Date: _____

Directions: *We can all learn from our successes and our mistakes. To complete this form, carefully reflect upon each piece in your portfolio. Think about the purpose for each sample of work. Examine your work to locate both places where you succeeded and areas you feel could be improved or further developed. Remember, you are assessing your own progress in the class. In order to enhance your learning experiences, you must be able to identify areas that you could improve upon.*

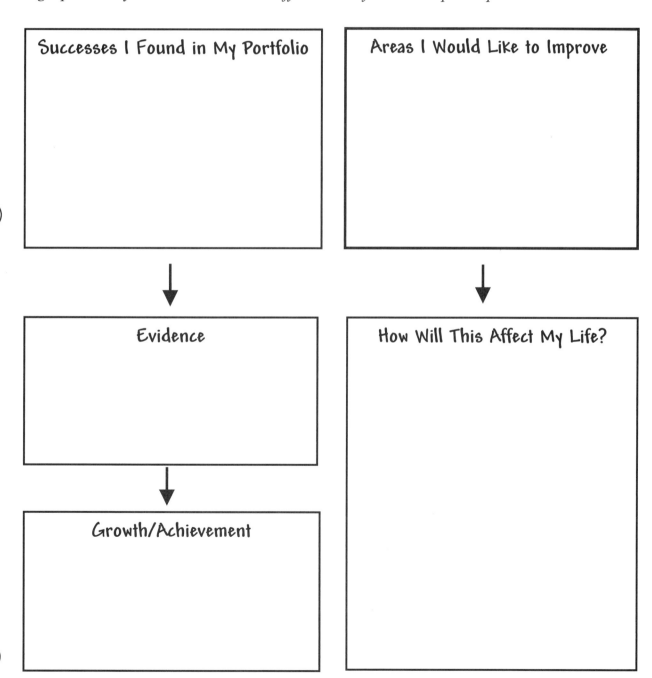

Successes I Found in My Portfolio	Areas I Would Like to Improve

Evidence

How Will This Affect My Life?

Growth/Achievement

Rubrics

Many teachers who work with gifted middle schoolers report success when using rubrics to help assess student achievement. A rubric is a scoring tool in which teachers list the criteria that they will be evaluating on a particular assignment. How many times do we as educators hear, "What will be graded on this project?" "Will grammar count for this assignment?" Criteria for assessing a piece of writing might include things like purpose, organization, voice, and mechanics. Rubrics have become popular among middle school teachers because they are powerful tools for assessment.

Rubrics can monitor student performance as well as improve it (Goodrich, 1997). Rubrics help to clarify teacher expectations by showing students how to meet certain criteria; when this happens, teachers report improvement in the quality of student work and learning. Rubrics also reduce the amount of time teachers spend on grading because students become more thoughtful about their work and typically make judgments and evaluations before turning their assignments in.

The following points will help as teachers begin using rubrics to assess student achievement (Andrade, 1997):

➤ Look at current models of successful rubrics to get a feeling for the framework and terminology used when preparing these tools.

➤ Begin by brainstorming a list of criteria that can be used for any subject or any project; this will help when searching for words to include on the rubric.

➤ Articulate gradations of quality, making sure to include descriptions of the best and worst levels of quality, as well as what would represent average quality.

It is wise to practice using rubrics with students before actually using a rubric to determine grades. This will help sort out any problems or misunderstandings. Provide time for self-assessment and peer assessment—i.e., give an assignment and then follow up with times for students to stop their work and either self-assess their progress or have a peer assess their progress. Always give time for students to revise their work. Be sure to use the same rubric you gave the students to assess the final product.

Using rubrics with gifted readers in middle school has many advantages. The most desirable outcomes will occur when students begin reflecting on each piece of work they turn in for a grade. They can judge for themselves whether they have reached the highest level of performance or an average level. They can then revise their work to include elements still needed to score in the higher range.

Encouraging students to reflect on personal progress allows them to take more responsibility for their learning. With a rubric, students are clear about expectations before they begin the assignment, and they can refer to the rubric as they work, revising more than once. Thus, using a performance-based assignment that is evaluated with a rubric promotes interaction between students and their learning.

Holistic Critical Thinking Scoring Rubric

Peter and Noreen Facione have developed the four-level *Holistic Critical Thinking Scoring Rubric* (1994) to assess critical thinking skills. It is copied on the next page and is available free of charge, with a full page of instructions, at:

www.insightassessment.com/pdf_files/Rubric%20HCTSR.pdf

The Holistic Critical Thinking Scoring Rubric

Strong **4**	Consistently does all or almost all of the following: ➤ Accurately interprets evidence, statements, graphics, questions, etc. ➤ Identifies the salient arguments (reasons and claims) pro and con ➤ Thoughtfully analyzes and evaluates major alternative points of view ➤ Draws warranted, judicious, non-fallacious conclusions ➤ Justifies key results and procedures, explains assumptions and reasons ➤ Fair-mindedly follows where evidence and reasons lead
Acceptable **3**	Does most or many of the following: ➤ Accurately interprets evidence, statements, graphics, questions, etc. ➤ Identifies relevant arguments (reasons and claims) pro and con ➤ Offers analyses and evaluations of obvious alternative points of view ➤ Draws warranted, non-fallacious conclusions ➤ Justifies some results or procedures, explains reasons ➤ Fair-mindedly follows where evidence and reasons lead
Unacceptable **2**	Does most or many of the following: ➤ Misinterprets evidence, statements, graphics, questions, etc. ➤ Fails to identify strong, relevant counter-arguments ➤ Ignores or superficially evaluates obvious alternative points of view ➤ Draws unwarranted or fallacious conclusions ➤ Justifies few results or procedures, seldom explains reasons ➤ Regardless of the evidence or reasons, maintains or defends views based on self-interest or preconceptions
Weak **1**	Consistently does all or almost all of the following: ➤ Offers biased interpretations of evidence, statements, graphics, questions, information, or the points of view of others ➤ Fails to identify or hastily dismisses strong, relevant counter-arguments ➤ Ignores or superficially evaluates obvious alternative points of view ➤ Argues using fallacious or irrelevant reasons and unwarranted claims ➤ Regardless of the evidence or reasons, maintains or defends views based on self-interest or preconceptions ➤ Exhibits close-mindedness or hostility to reason

Reprinted from Facione & Facione, 1994.

✐ Key Points

1. Assessment drives curriculum; therefore teachers need to choose assessment methods that are effective in providing information related to students' progress.

2. Assessment should be an ongoing process and not just a single snapshot of a student's ability.

3. There are many different methods for assessing gifted readers in middle school. These include self-assessment, peer assessment, student conferences, portfolios, and rubrics.

4. Gifted readers in middle school should be given opportunities to assess themselves and reflect upon this information in order to make needed changes.

References

Aiex, N. K. (1993). *Bibliotherapy.* ERIC Document Reproduction Service No. ED357333.

Anchor activities. (2000). Retrieved May 25, 2010, from www.teach.virginia.edu/files/nagc_anchor_activities.pdf

Andrade, H. (1997). Understanding rubrics. *Educational Leadership, 54,* 4-8.

Atwell, N. (2007). *The reading zone: How to help kids become skilled, passionate, habitual, critical readers.* New York: Scholastic Professional Books.

Austin, P. (2003). Challenging gifted readers. *Book Links, 4*(2), 32-37.

Bernstein, H. T. (1985). The new politics of textbook adoption. *Phi Delta Kappan, 66*(7), 463-646.

Bloom, B. S. (1956). *Taxonomy of educational objectives: The classification of educational goals. Handbook I: Cognitive domain.* New York: Layman.

Bruzzese, J. (2009). *A parent's guide to the middle school years.* Berkeley, CA: Celestial Arts.

Buescher, T. M., & Higham, S. (1985). *Helping adolescents adjust to giftedness.* ERIC Document Reproduction Service No. E489.

Chall, J., & Conrad, W. (1991). *Should textbooks challenge students? The case for easier or harder textbooks.* New York: Teachers College Press.

Clark, B. (2008), *Growing up gifted: Developing the potential of children at home and at school* (7th ed.). Upper Saddle River, NJ: Pearson/Merrill Prentice Hall.

Codd, M. (1999). *The social and emotional development of gifted children.* Barrington, RI: Rhode Island Advocates for Gifted Education.

Creech, S. (1994). *Walk two moons.* New York: HarperCollins.

Cushman, K. (1995). *The midwife's apprentice.* New York: Clarion Books.

Delisle, J. (1985). Counseling gifted persons: A lifelong concern. *Roeper Review, 8*(1), 4-5.

Delisle, J. (1991). *Guiding the social and emotional development of gifted youth: A practical guide for educators and counselors.* New York: Longman.

Edwards, S., & Simpson, H. (1986). A strategy for communicating between parents and their children. *Journal of Reading, 30*(2), 101-108.

Facione, P. A., & Facione, N. C. (1994). *The holistic critical thinking scoring rubric: A tool for developing and evaluating critical thinking.* Retrieved May 24, 2010, from www.insightassessment.com/pdf_files/Rubric%20HCTSR.pdf

Fay, L., Humphrey, J., & Smith, C. (2006). Young adolescent literacy or young adolescent reading: They are not the same. *Indiana Reading Journal, 38*(1), 9-12.

Gilman, B. J. (2008). *Academic advocacy for gifted children: A parent's complete guide.* Scottsdale, AZ: Great Potential Press.

Goodrich, H. (1997). Understanding rubrics. *Educational Leadership, 54*(4), 32-39.

Grobman, J. (2006). Underachievement in exceptionally gifted adolescents and young adults: A psychiatrist's view. *The Journal of Secondary Education, 17*(4), 199-210.

Halsted, J. W. (2009). *Some of my best friends are books: Guiding gifted readers from preschool to high school* (3rd ed.). Scottsdale, AZ: Great Potential Press.

Heacox, D. (2002). *Differentiating instruction in the regular classroom: How to reach and teach all learners grades 3-12.* Minneapolis, MN: Free Spirit.

Hébert, T. P., & Kent R. (2000). Nurturing social and emotional development in gifted teenagers through young adult literature. *Roeper Review, 22*(3), 167-171.

Kimeldore, M. (1994). *Creating portfolios for success in school, work, and life.* Minneapolis, MN: Free Spirit.

Kingore, B. (2002). *Reading strategies for advanced primary readers.* Austin, TX: Texas Educational Agency.

Larkin, M. J. (2001). Providing support for student independence through scaffold instruction. *Teaching Exceptional Children, 34*(1), 30-36.

Levande, D. (1999). Gifted readers and reading instruction. *CAG Communicator, 30*(1), 21-25.

Lobel, A. (1998). *No pretty pictures: A child of war.* New York: Greenwillow Books.

Masiello, T. S. (2007). *Understanding the social and emotional needs of gifted adolescents: An informal survey identifying the needs of gifted students in middle school.* Unpublished manuscript.

Maslow, A. H. (1998). *Toward a psychology of being* (3rd ed.). New York: Wiley & Sons.

Monseau, V., & Salvner G. (2000). *Reading their world: The young adult novel in the classroom* (2nd ed.). Portsmouth, NH: Boynton & Cook.

National Association for Gifted Children. (2010). *Redefining giftedness for a new century: Shifting the paradigm.* Retrieved May 17, 2010, from www.nagc.org/uploadedFiles/About_NAGC/Redefining%20Giftedness%20for%20a%20New%20Century.pdf

National Middle School Association. (2010). *This we believe: Successful schools for young adolescents.* Westerville, OH: Author.

North American Division Office of Education. (2010). *Socratic seminars.* Retrieved June 3, 2010, from www.journeytoexcellence.org/practice/instruction/theories/miscideas/socratic

Osborne, J. (2001). *Issues in educating exceptionally gifted students.* Retrieved May 28, 2010, from www.davidsongifted.org/db/Articles_id_10208.aspx

Painter, J. (1996). Questioning techniques for gifted students. *The Educational Technology Journal, 7*(3), 45-48.

Paulsen, G. (1997). *The Schernoff discoveries.* New York: Delacorte Press.

Perie, M., Grigg, W., & Donahue, P. (2005). *The nation's report card: Reading 2005.* (NCES 2006-451). Washington, DC: U.S. Department of Education, National Center for Education Statistics.

Rakow, S. (2005). *Educating gifted students in middle school: A practical guide.* Waco, TX: Prufrock Press.

Reis, S. M., & McCoach, D. B. (2000). The underachievement of gifted students: What do we know and where do we go? *Gifted Child Quarterly, 44*(3), 152-170.

Reis, S. M., & Renzulli, J. S. (2005). *Curriculum compacting: An easy start to differentiating instruction high potential students.* Waco, TX: Prufrock Press.

Richards, S. (2008). Beyond the Caldecott and Newbery: Awards and lists of books for the active reader and thinker. *Gifted Education Communicator, 39*(4), 48-50.

Rimm, S. B. (2008). *Why bright kids get poor grades and what you can do about it.* Scottsdale, AZ: Great Potential Press.

Rogers, K. B. (2002). *Re-forming gifted education: How parents and teachers can match the program to the child.* Scottsdale, AZ: Great Potential Press.

Rogers, K. B. (2006). *A menu of options for grouping gifted students.* Waco, TX: Prufrock Press.

Ross, E., & Wright, J. (1985). *Teaching strategies to fit the learning styles of gifted readers in middle school.* ERIC Document Reproduction Service No. ED262388.

Ruf, D. (2005). *5 Levels of gifted: School issues and educational options.* Scottsdale, AZ: Great Potential Press.

Siegle, D., & Schuler, P. (2000). Perfectionism and differences in gifted middle school students. *Roeper Review, 23*(1), 39-44.

Smutny, J. F. (2000). *Stand up for your gifted child: How to make the most of kids' strengths at school and at home.* Minneapolis, MN: Free Spirit.

Strip, C. A., with Hirsch, G. (2000). *Helping gifted children soar.* Scottsdale, AZ: Great Potential Press.

StudyGuide.org. (2009). *Socratic seminars.* Retrieved June 3, 2010, from www.studyguide.org/socratic_seminar.htm

Taylor, B. M., & Frye, B. J. (1988). Pretesting: Minimize time spent on skill work for intermediate readers. *Reading Teacher, 42*(2), 100-104.

Tomlinson, C. (2001). *How to differentiate in mixed-ability classrooms* (2nd ed.). Alexandria, VA: Association for Supervision and Curriculum Development.

Tomlinson, C. (2003). *Fulfilling the promise of the differentiated classroom: Strategies and tools for responsive teaching.* Alexandria, VA: Association for Supervision and Curriculum Development.

Tredway, L. (n.d.) *Socratic seminars: Engaging students in intellectual discourse.* Retrieved April 26, 2010, from www.middleweb.com/Socratic.html

Valentino, C. (2000). *Flexible grouping.* Retrieved May 13, 2010, from www.eduplace.com/science/profdev/articles/valentino.html

VanTassel-Baska, J. (2002). *Planning effective curriculum experiences for gifted learners.* Retrieved May 28, 2010, from www.davidsongifted.org/db/Articles_id_10278.aspx

Webb, J. T., Gore, J. L., Amend, E. R., & DeVries, A. R. (2007). *A parent's guide to gifted children.* Scottsdale, AZ: Great Potential Press.

Whitney, C. S., with Hirsch, G. (2007). *A love for learning: Motivation and the gifted child.* Scottsdale, AZ: Great Potential Press.

Willis, J. A. (2009). *Inspiring middle school minds: Gifted, creative, and challenging.* Scottsdale, AZ: Great Potential Press.

Winebrenner, S. (2001). *Teaching gifted kids in the regular classroom.* Minneapolis, MN: Free Spirit.

Index

About the Author

Teresa Masiello is the assessment specialist for learning at Shenandoah University, located in Winchester, Virginia. Prior positions include teaching kindergarten in Fairfax County, Virginia, and first through fifth grades in Fredrick County, Virginia. Her 24 years of teaching experience include work in gifted education, assessment, and curriculum. Teresa also spent several years at the middle school level providing enrichment for students identified as being gifted and talented.

Teresa earned a bachelor's degree in elementary education from George Mason University and a master's degree in teaching from Shenandoah University. Over time, she also earned endorsements in gifted education, administration, and supervision. She has received a Doctor of Education degree from Shenandoah University.

For many years, Teresa has been a frequent speaker, consultant, and workshop presenter on gifted education topics to audiences throughout the United States. She published *Literature Links: Activities for Gifted Readers* in 2005. She continues to conduct research that relates to gifted education and higher education. She conducted at study at Shenandoah University that identifies best practices when creating intentional learning communities in colleges and universities. Results from this study help faculty members determine how to best meet the needs of students who are members of a learning community. Other research topics include assessment in higher education and meeting the needs of the millennials. Teresa currently writes grants for Shenandoah University, as well as develops appropriate curriculum for first-year students.

When not presenting at national conferences for gifted children, Teresa spends time with her family. She and her husband Paul have been married for 22 years. They enjoy spending time with their 17-year-old son Anthony and 12-year-old twins Jacob and Nicole. Teresa acknowledges that her parents, Marshall and Cecilia Smith, instilled a strong desire to establish goals and continue lifelong learning when she was a child. She is thankful to have such a supportive family and parents who vested time and energy into her education.